Building Act 1984

CHAPTER 55

Explanatory Notes are available separately

GRANG*IS* UK Publishing

Adapted and published by GRANGIS (Grand Register Library).
Online: www.grangis.com
E-mail: contact@grangis.com

In this version:
ISBN: 979-8-88559-053-2

Note: This is the original version (as it was originally enacted). Title, sub-title and the generated date is as marked on the pages.

Building Act 1984

CHAPTER 55

BUILDING ACT 1984

PART I

BUILDING REGULATIONS

Power to make building regulations

Exemption from building regulations

Approved documents

Relaxation of building regulations

Type approval of building matter

Consultation

Passing of plans

Determination of questions

Proposed departure from plans

Lapse of deposit of plans

Tests for conformity with building regulations

Classification of buildings

Breach of building regulations

Appeals in certain cases

Entry on premises

Execution of works

Appeal against notice requiring works

General provisions about appeals and applications

Compensation, and recovery of sums

Obstruction

Prosecutions

Protection of members etc. of authorities

Default powers

Local inquiries

Orders

Interpretation

Savings

PART V

SUPPLEMENTARY

SCHEDULES

Application of Schedule

Cases where no direction may be given

SCHEDULE 5 — Transitional Provisions

Joint application to the Secretary of State for the determination of certain questions relating to building regulations

1 After the date on which section 30 of this Act...

The Clean Air Act 1956 and the Housing Act 1957

2 Notwithstanding the repeal by this Act of Schedule 1 to...

Repeal and amendment of Acts etc.

3 Any power that is exercisable by virtue of—
4 (1) Section 64(5) of the Act of 1936, in so...
5 Without prejudice to the power to make building regulations, the...

SCHEDULE 6 — Consequential Amendments

The Restriction of Ribbon Development Act 1935

1 In section 17(1) of the Restriction of Ribbon Development Act...

The Public Health Act 1936

2 In section 6(1) of the Public Health Act 1936, after...
3 In section 269(8)(i) of that Act, for " the building...

The Atomic Energy Authority Act 1954

4 In section 5(5) of the Atomic Energy Authority Act 1954,...

The Clean Air Act 1956

5 In section 10(2) of the Clean Air Act 1956, for...

The Housing Act 1957

6 In section 15(1)(b) of the Housing Act 1957, after "...

The Radioactive Substances Act 1960

7 At the end of Part I of Schedule 1 to...

The Public Health Act 1961

8 In section 17(15) of the Public Health Act 1961 (as...

The London Government Act 1963

9 In paragraph 19 of Part I of Schedule 11 to...
10 In paragraph 9(5) of Part II of Schedule 11 to...

The Offices, Shops and Railway Premises Act 1963

11 In section 9(6) of the Offices, Shops and Railway Premises...

The Faculty Jurisdiction Measure 1964

12 In section 2(4) of the Faculty Jurisdiction Measure 1964—

The Fire Precautions Act 1971

13 For section 30(3)(a) and (b) of the Fire Precautions Act...

The Local Government Act 1972

14 In section 181(2)(a) of the Local Government Act 1972, for...

The Safety of Sports Grounds Act 1975

15 In section 9(1)(c) of the Safety of Sports Grounds Act...

The Local Land Charges Act 1975

16 In section 1(1)(a) of the Local Land Charges Act 1975,...

The Local Government (Miscellaneous Provisions) Act 1976

17 In section 12(3) of the Local Government (Miscellaneous Provisions) Act...

The Development of Rural Wales Act 1976

18 In paragraph 51(3) of Schedule 3 to the Development of...

The Interpretation Act 1978

19 In Schedule 1 to the Interpretation Act 1978, in the...

The Highways Act 1980

20 In section 168(1)(b) of the Highways Act 1980, for "...
21 In section 223(1)(a) of that Act, for " section 66...

New Towns Act 1981

22 In section 34(3) of the New Towns Act 1981—

The Public Health (Control of Disease) Act 1984

23 There is added at the end of section 7(4) of...

SCHEDULE 7 — Repeals

TABLE OF — DERIVATIONS

1 Notes:
2 The following abbreviations are used in this Table: 1875 =...

Building Act 1984

1984 CHAPTER 55

An Act to consolidate certain enactments concerning building and buildings and related matters. [31st October 1984]

BE IT ENACTED by the Queen's most Excellent Majesty, by and with the advice and consent of the Lords Spiritual and Temporal, and Commons, in this present Parliament assembled, and by the authority of the same, as follows:—

PART I

BUILDING REGULATIONS

Power to make building regulations

1 Power to make building regulations

(1) The Secretary of State may, for any of the purposes of—

(a) securing the health, safety, welfare and convenience of persons in or about buildings and of others who may be affected by buildings or matters connected with buildings,

(b) furthering the conservation of fuel and power, and

(c) preventing waste, undue consumption, misuse or contamination of water,

make regulations with respect to the design and construction of buildings and the provision of services, fittings and equipment in or in connection with buildings.

(2) Regulations made under subsection (1) above are known as building regulations.

(3) Schedule 1 to this Act has effect with respect to the matters as to which building regulations may provide.

(4) The power to make building regulations is exercisable by statutory instrument, which is subject to annulment in pursuance of a resolution of either House of Parliament.

2 Continuing requirements

(1) Building regulations may impose on owners and occupiers of buildings to which building regulations are applicable such continuing requirements as the Secretary of State considers appropriate for securing, with respect to any provision of building regulations designated in the regulations as a provision to which those requirements relate, that the purposes of that provision, are not frustrated; but a continuing requirement imposed by virtue of this subsection does not apply in relation to a building unless a provision of building regulations so designated as one to which the requirement relates applies to that building.

(2) Building regulations may impose on owners and occupiers of buildings of a prescribed class (whenever erected, and whether or not any building regulations were applicable to them at the time of their erection) continuing requirements with respect to all or any of the following matters—

- (a) the conditions subject to which any services, fittings or equipment provided in or in connection with a building of that class may be used,
- (b) the inspection and maintenance of any services, fittings or equipment so provided,
- (c) the making of reports to a prescribed authority on the condition of any services, fittings or equipment so provided,

and so much of paragraph 8 of Schedule 1 to this Act as restricts the application of building regulations does not apply to regulations made by virtue of this subsection.

(3) If a person contravenes a continuing requirement imposed by virtue of this section, the local authority, without prejudice to their right to take proceedings for a fine in respect of the contravention, may—

- (a) execute any work or take any other action required to remedy the contravention, and
- (b) recover from that person the expenses reasonably incurred by them in so doing.

(4) Where a local authority have power under subsection (3) above to execute any work or take any other action, they may, instead of exercising that power, by notice require the owner or the occupier of the building to which the contravention referred to in that subsection relates to execute that work or take that action.

(5) Sections 99 and 102 below apply in relation to a notice given under subsection (4) above, subject to the modification that references in those sections to the execution of works are references to the execution of works or the taking of other action, and references to works shall be construed accordingly.

(6) Sections 8, 9, 10 and 39 below have effect in relation to continuing requirements imposed by virtue of this section subject to the modification that a direction under the said sections 8 and 9 below shall, if it so provides, cease to have effect at the end of such period as may be specified in the direction.

Exemption from building regulations

3 Exemption of particular classes of buildings etc.

(1) Building regulations may exempt a prescribed class of buildings, services, fittings or equipment from all or any of the provisions of building regulations.

(2) The Secretary of State may by direction exempt from all or any of the provisions of building regulations—

(a) a particular building, or

(b) buildings of a particular class at a particular location,

either unconditionally or subject to compliance with any conditions specified in the direction.

(3) A person who contravenes a condition specified in a direction given under subsection (2) above, or permits such a condition to be contravened, is liable on summary conviction to a fine not exceeding level 5 on the standard scale, and to a further fine not exceeding £50 for each day on which the offence continues after he is convicted.

4 Exemption of educational buildings and buildings of statutory undertakers

(1) Nothing in this Part of this Act with respect to building regulations, and nothing in any building regulations, applies in relation to—

(a) a building required for the purposes of a school or other educational establishment erected or to be erected according to plans that have been approved by the Secretary of State for Education and Science or the Secretary of State for Wales, or according to particulars submitted to and approved by the Secretary of State under section 14 of the Education Act 1980 or under regulations made under section 27(4) of that Act, or

(b) a building belonging to statutory undertakers, the United Kingdom Atomic Energy Authority, the British Airports Authority or the Civil Aviation Authority and held or used by them for the purposes of their undertaking, unless it is—

(i) a house, or in the case of the British Airports Authority a house or a hotel, or

(i) a building used as offices or showrooms, and not forming part of a railway station or in the case of the British Airports Authority or the Civil Aviation Authority not being on an aerodrome owned by the Authority in question.

(2) The words " the United Kingdom Atomic Energy Authority," in subsection (1)(b) above (together with paragraph 4 of Schedule 6 to this Act) cease to have effect upon the coming into force of the repeal of section 5(5) of the Atomic Energy Authority Act 1954 contained in Schedule 7 to this Act.

5 Exemption of public bodies from procedural requirements of building regulations

(1) Building regulations may exempt—

(a) a local authority,

(b) a county council, or

(c) any other body that acts under an enactment for public purposes and not for its own profit and is prescribed for the purposes of this section,

from compliance with any requirements of those regulations that are not substantive requirements.

(2) A local authority, county council or other body that is exempted as mentioned in subsection (1) above is in subsection (3) below referred to as an " exempt body ".

(3) Without prejudice to the obligation of an exempt body to comply with substantive requirements of building regulations, the function of enforcing building regulations that is conferred on local authorities by section 91(2) below is not exercisable in relation to work carried out by an exempt body, and accordingly—

(a) nothing in section 36(1) to (5) below applies in relation to work so carried out, and

(b) a local authority may not institute proceedings under section 35 below for a contravention of building regulations by an exempt body.

(4) In subsection (3) above, the reference to the carrying out of work includes a reference to the making of a material change of use as defined by and for the purposes of building regulations.

Approved documents

6 Approval of documents for purposes of building regulations

(1) For the purpose of providing practical guidance with respect to the requirements of any provision of building regulations, the Secretary of State or a body designated by him for the purposes of this section may—

(a) approve and issue any document (whether or not prepared by him or by the body concerned), or

(b) approve any document issued or proposed to be issued otherwise than by him or by the body concerned,

if in the opinion of the Secretary of State or, as the case may be, the body concerned the document is suitable for that purpose.

(2) References in this section and section 7 below to a document include references to a part of a document; and accordingly, in relation to a document of which part only is approved, a reference in the following provisions of this section or in section 7 below to the approved document is a reference only to the part of it that is approved.

(3) An approval given under subsection (1) above takes effect in accordance with a notice that is issued by the Secretary of State or, as the case may be, the body giving the approval and that—

(a) identifies the approved document in question,

(b) states the date on which the approval of it is to take effect, and

(c) specifies the provisions of building regulations for the purposes of which the document is approved.

(4) The Secretary of State or, as the case may be, the body that gave the approval may—

(a) from time to time approve and issue a revision of the whole or any part of an approved document issued by him or it for the purposes of this section, and

(b) approve any revision or proposed revision of the whole or any part of an approved document,

and subsection (3) above, with the necessary modifications, applies in relation to an approval that is given under this subsection to a revision as it applies in relation to an approval that is given under subsection (1) above to a document.

(5) The Secretary of State or, as the case may be, the body that gave the approval may withdraw his or its approval of a document under this section; and such a withdrawal

of approval takes effect in accordance with a notice that is issued by the Secretary of State or body concerned and that—

(a) identifies the approved document in question, and

(b) states the date on which the approval of it is to cease to have effect.

(6) References in subsections (4) and (5) above and in section 7 below to an approved document are references to that document as it has effect for the time being, regard being had to any revision of the whole or any part of it that has been approved under subsection (4) above.

(7) Where a body ceases to be a body designated by the Secretary of State for the purposes of this section, subsections (4) and (5) above have effect as if any approval given by that body had been given by the Secretary of State.

(8) The power to designate a body for the purposes of this section is exercisable by order made by statutory instrument, which is subject to annulment in pursuance of a resolution of either House of Parliament.

7 Compliance or non-compliance with approved documents

(1) A failure on the part of a person to comply with an approved document does not of itself render him liable to any civil or criminal proceedings ; but if, in any proceedings whether civil or criminal, it is alleged that a person has at any time contravened a provision of building regulations—

(a) a failure to comply with a document that at that time was approved for the purposes of that provision may be relied upon as tending to establish liability, and

(b) proof of compliance with such a document may be relied on as tending to negative liability.

(2) In any proceedings, whether civil or criminal—

(a) a document purporting to be a notice issued as mentioned in section 6(3) above shall be taken to be such a notice unless the contrary is proved, and

(b) a document that appears to the court to be the approved document to which such a notice refers shall be taken to be that approved document unless the contrary is proved.

Relaxation of building regulations

8 Relaxation of building regulations

(1) Subject to this section, the Secretary of State, if on an application for a direction under this section he considers that the operation of a requirement in building regulations would be unreasonable hi relation to the particular case to which the application relates, may, after consultation with the local authority, give a direction dispensing with or relaxing that requirement

(2) If building regulations so provide as regards a requirement contained in the regulations, the power to dispense with or relax that requirement under subsection (1) above is exercisable by the local authority (instead of by the Secretary of State after consultation with the local authority).

(3) Building regulations made by virtue of subsection (2) above may except applications of any description.

(4) If—

(a) building regulations so provide as regards any requirement contained in the regulations, and

(b) a public body considers that the operation of any such requirement would be unreasonable in relation to any particular work carried out or proposed to be carried out by or on behalf of the public body,

the public body may give a direction dispensing with or relaxing that requirement.

(5) In subsection (4) above, " public body " means—

(a) a local authority,

(b) a county council, or

(c) any other body that is prescribed for the purposes of section 5 above.

(6) Building regulations may provide as regards a requirement contained in the regulations that subsections (1) to (5) above do not apply.

9 Application for relaxation

(1) An application under section 8(1) or (2) above shall be in such form and shall contain such particulars as may be prescribed.

(2) The application shall be made to the local authority, and, except where the power of giving the direction is exercisable by the local authority, the local authority shall at once transmit the application to the Secretary of State and give notice to the applicant that it has been so transmitted.

(3) An application by a local authority in connection with a building or proposed building in the area of that authority shall be made to the Secretary of State, except where the power of giving the direction is exercisable by that authority.

(4) Schedule 2 to this Act has effect as regards an application for a direction that will affect the application of building regulations to work that has been carried out before the making of the application.

10 Advertisement of proposal for relaxation of building regulations

(1) Not less than 21 days before giving a direction under section 8(1), (2) or (4) above in respect of any particular work, the Secretary of State, the local authority or the public body, as the case may be, shall publish in a local newspaper circulating in the area where the site of the work is situated a notice—

(a) indicating the situation and nature of the work and the requirement to be dispensed with or relaxed, and

(b) stating that representations with regard to the effect that the direction may have on public health or safety may be made by a date specified in the notice, being a date not less than 21 days from the date of the notice,

and, where the direction is proposed to be made on an application, the Secretary of State or the local authority may, as a condition of entertaining the application, require the applicant to pay or undertake to pay the cost of publication.

(2) No notice need be published under subsection (1) above where it appears to the Secretary of State, the local authority or the public body, as the case may be, that any effect that the direction may have on public health or safety will be limited to premises adjoining the site of the work, but in that case he, they or it shall give such a notice to the owner and occupier of those premises.

(3) No notice need be published or given under subsection (1) or (2) above where the work affects only an internal part of a building.

(4) The Secretary of State may, instead of himself publishing or giving a notice under subsection (1) or (2) above, require the local authority to give or publish the notice.

(5) Before giving the direction, the Secretary of State, the local authority or the public body shall consider any representations duly made in pursuance of a notice published or given under subsection (1) or (2) above.

(6) If, after a local authority have received representations under this section, they refuse the application to which the representations relate and an appeal is brought against their refusal, the local authority shall transmit to the Secretary of State copies of those representations.

11 Type relaxation of building regulations

(1) If the Secretary of State considers that the operation of a requirement of building regulations would be unreasonable in relation to a particular type of building matter, he may, either on an application made to him or of his own accord, give a direction dispensing with or relaxing that requirement generally in relation to that type of building matter, either—

(a) unconditionally, or

(b) subject to compliance with any conditions specified in the direction, being conditions with respect to matters directly connected with the dispensation or relaxation.

(2) A direction under subsection (1) above—

(a) if it so provides, ceases to have effect at the end of such period as may be specified in the direction,

(b) may be varied or revoked by a subsequent direction of the Secretary of State.

(3) Building regulations may require a person making an application under subsection (1) above to pay the Secretary of State the prescribed fee, and—

(a) without prejudice to paragraph 10 of Schedule 1 to this Act, regulations made by virtue of this subsection may prescribe different fees for different cases, and

(b) the Secretary of State may in a particular case remit the whole or part of a fee payable by virtue of this subsection.

(4) Before giving a direction under subsection (1) above, the Secretary of State shall consult such bodies as appear to him to be representative of the interests concerned.

(5) Where the Secretary of State gives a direction under subsection (1) above, he shall publish notice of that fact in such manner as he thinks fit.

(6) A person who contravenes a condition specified in a direction given under subsection (1) above, or permits such a condition to be contravened, is liable on

summary conviction to a fine not exceeding level 5 on the standard scale and to a further fine not exceeding £50 for each day on which the offence continues after he is convicted.

(7) If at any time a direction under subsection (1) above dispensing with or relaxing a requirement of building regulations ceases to have effect by virtue of subsection (2)(a) above, or is varied or revoked under subsection (2)(b) above, that fact does not affect the continued operation of the direction (with any conditions specified in it) in a case in which before that time—

(a) plans of the proposed work were, in accordance with building regulations, deposited with a local authority, or

(b) a building notice was served on the district surveyor in pursuance of section 83 of the London Building Acts (Amendment) Act 1939.

(8) In this section, " building matter " means any building or other matter whatsoever to which building regulations are in any circumstances applicable.

Type approval of building matter

12 Power of Secretary of State to approve type of building matter

(1) This section has effect with a view to enabling the Secretary of State, either on an application made to him or of his own accord, to approve a particular type of building matter as complying, either generally or in a class of case, with particular requirements of building regulations.

(2) An application for the approval under subsection (1) above of a type of building matter shall comply with any requirements of building regulations as to the form of such applications and the particulars to be included in them.

(3) Where under subsection (1) above the Secretary of State approves a type of building matter as complying with particular requirements of building regulations either generally or in a class of case, he may issue a certificate to that effect specifying—

(a) the type of building matter to which the certificate relates,

(b) the requirements of building regulations to which the certificate relates, and

(c) where applicable, the class or classes of case to which the certificate applies.

(4) A certificate under subsection (3) above, if it so provides, ceases to have effect at the end of such period as may be specified in the certificate.

(5) If, while a certificate under subsection (3) above is in force, it is found, in a particular case involving building matter of the type to which the certificate relates, that—

(a) the building matter in question is of that type, and

(b) the case is one to which the certificate applies,

that building matter shall in that particular case be deemed to comply with the requirements of building regulations to which the certificate relates.

(6) The Secretary of State may vary a certificate under subsection (3) above, either on an application made to him or of his own accord; but, in the case of a certificate issued on an application made by a person Under subsection (1) above, the Secretary of State, except where he varies it on the application of that person, shall before varying it give that person reasonable notice that he proposes to do so.

(7) Building regulations may require a person making an application under subsection (1) or (6) above to pay the Secretary of State the prescribed fee, and—

(a) without prejudice to paragraph 10 of Schedule 1 to this Act, regulations made by virtue of this subsection may prescribe different fees for different cases, and

(b) the Secretary of State may in a particular case remit the whole or part of a fee payable by virtue of this subsection.

(8) The Secretary of State may revoke a certificate issued under subsection (3) above, but, before doing so in the case of a certificate issued on an application under subsection (1) above, he shall give the person on whose application the certificate was issued reasonable notice that he proposes to do so.

(9) Where the Secretary of State issues a certificate under subsection (3) above or varies or revokes a certificate so issued, he shall publish notice of that fact in such manner as he thinks fit

(10) If at any time a certificate under subsection (3) above ceases to have effect by virtue of subsection (4) above, or is varied or revoked under subsection (6) or (8) above, that fact does not affect the continued operation of subsection (5) above by virtue of that certificate in a case in which before that time—

(a) plans of the proposed work were, in accordance with building regulations, deposited with a local authority, or

(b) a building notice was served on the district surveyor in pursuance of section 83 of the London Building Acts (Amendment) Act 1939.

(11) For the purposes of subsection (3) above, or of any variation of a certificate under subsection (6) above, a class of case may be framed in any way that the Secretary of State thinks fit.

(12) In this section, " building matter " has the same meaning as in section 11 above.

13 Delegation of power to approve

(1) The Secretary of State may by building regulations delegate to a person or body, to such extent and subject to such conditions as the Secretary of State may think fit, the powers of approval conferred on him by section 12 above.

(2) So far as those powers are for the time being so delegated to a person or body, section 12 above, except subsection (7) as far as the end of paragraph (a), and any building regulations made by virtue of subsection (7) shall (subject to any prescribed conditions) have effect in relation to that person or body with the substitution of references to that person or body for references to the Secretary of State.

Consultation

14 Consultation with Building Regulations Advisory Committee and other bodies

(1) The Secretary of State for the time being charged with the exercise of the power to make building regulations and the Secretary of State for Wales acting jointly shall appoint a committee, to be known as the Building Regulations Advisory Committee, for the purpose of advising the Secretary of State on the exercise of his power to make building regulations, and on other subjects connected with building regulations.

(2) The Secretary of State may pay such expenses incurred by members of the Building Regulations Advisory Committee as he may, with the approval of the Treasury, determine.

(3) Before making any building regulations containing substantive requirements, the Secretary of State shall consult the Building Regulations Advisory Committee and such other bodies as appear to him to be representative of the interests concerned.

15 Consultation with fire authority

(1) Where, in the case of a requirement as to—

- (a) structural fire precautions,
- (b) the provision of means of escape from buildings in case of fire, or
- (c) the provision of means for securing that such means of escape can be safely and effectively used at all material times,

contained in building regulations, the power to dispense with or relax that requirement conferred by section 8(1) above is by virtue of section 8(2) above exercisable by a local authority, or a public body proposes to exercise the power conferred on it by section 8(4) above, the local authority or public body, if they are not the fire authority, shall before exercising the power in relation to any premises or proposed premises consult the fire authority.

(2) In subsection (1) above, " public body " has the meaning given by section 8(5) above.

Passing of plans

16 Passing or rejection of plans

(1) Where plans of any proposed work are, in accordance with building regulations, deposited with a local authority, it is the duty of the local authority, subject to any other section of this Act that expressly requires or authorises them in certain cases to reject plans, to pass the plans unless—

- (a) they are defective, or
- (b) they show that the proposed work would contravene any of the building regulations.

(2) If the plans—

- (a) are defective, or
- (b) show that the proposed work would contravene any of the building regulations,

the local authority may—

- (i) reject the plans, or
- (ii) subject to subsection (4) below, pass them subject to either or both of the conditions set out in subsection (3) below.

(3) The conditions mentioned in subsection (2) above are—

- (a) that such modifications as the local authority may specify shall be made in the deposited plans, and
- (b) that such further plans as they may specify shall be deposited.

(4) A local authority may only pass plans subject to a condition such as is specified in subsection (3) above if the person by whom or on whose behalf they were deposited—

(a) has requested them to do so, or

(b) has consented to their doing so.

(5) A request or consent under subsection (4) above shall be in writing.

(6) The authority shall within the relevant period from the deposit of the plans give notice to the person by whom or on whose behalf they were deposited whether they have been passed or rejected.

(7) A notice that plans have been rejected shall specify the defects on account of which, or the regulation or section of this Act for non-conformity with which, or under the authority of which, they have been rejected.

(8) A notice that plans have been passed shall—

(a) specify any condition subject to which they have been passed, and

(b) state that the passing of the plans operates as an approval of them only for the purposes of the requirements of—

(i) the building regulations, and

(ii) any section of this Act (other than this section) that expressly requires or authorises the local authority in certain cases to reject plans.

(9) Where the deposited plans are accompanied by—

(a) a certificate given by a person approved for the purposes of this subsection to the effect that the proposed work, if carried out in accordance with the deposited plans, will comply with such provisions of the regulations prescribed for the purposes of this subsection as may be specified in the certificate, and

(b) such evidence as may be prescribed that an approved scheme applies, or the prescribed insurance cover has been or will be provided, in relation to the certificate,

the local authority may not, except in prescribed circumstances, reject the plans on the ground that—

(i) they are defective with respect to any provisions of the building regulations that are so specified, or

(ii) they show that the proposed work would contravene any of those provisions.

(10) In any case where a question arises under this section between a local authority and a person who proposes to carry out any work—

(a) whether plans of the proposed work are in conformity with building regulations, or

(b) whether the local authority are prohibited from rejecting plans of the proposed work by virtue of subsection (9) above,

that person may refer the question to the Secretary of State for his determination ; and an application for a reference under this subsection shall be accompanied by such fee as may be prescribed.

(11) Where—

(a) deposited plans accompanied by such a certificate and such evidence as are mentioned in subsection (9) above are passed by the local authority, or

(b) notice of the rejection of deposited plans so accompanied is not given within the relevant period from the deposit of the plans,

the authority may not institute proceedings under section 35 below for a contravention of building regulations that—

(i) arises out of the carrying out of the proposed work in accordance with the plans, and

(ii) is a contravention of any of the provisions of the regulations specified in the certificate.

(12) For the purposes of this Part of this Act, " the relevant period ", in relation to the passing or rejection of plans, means five weeks or such extended period (expiring not later than two months from the deposit of the plans) as may before the expiration of the five weeks be agreed in writing between the person depositing the plans and the local authority.

(13) Until such day as the Secretary of State may by order appoint, subsection (10) above has effect as follows—

"(10) Any question arising under this section between a local authority and the person by whom or on whose behalf plans are deposited as to whether the plans are defective, or whether the proposed work would contravene any of the regulations, may on the application of that person be determined by a magistrates' court, but no such application shall be entertained unless it is made before the proposed work has been substantially commenced."

17 Approval of persons to give certificates etc.

(1) Building regulations may make provision for the approval of persons for the purposes of section 16(9) above—

(a) by the Secretary of State, or

(b) by a body (corporate or unincorporated) that, in accordance with the regulations, is designated by the Secretary of State for the purpose,

and any such approval may limit the description of work, or the provisions of the regulations, in relation to which the person concerned is so approved.

(2) Any such designation as is referred to in paragraph (b) of subsection (1) above may limit the cases in which and the terms on which the body designated may approve a person and, in particular, may provide that any approval given by the body shall be limited as mentioned in that subsection.

(3) There shall be paid on an application for any such approval as is referred to in subsection (1) above—

(a) where the application is made to the Secretary of State, such fee as may be prescribed,

(b) where the application is made to a body designated by him as mentioned in that subsection, such fee as that body may determine.

(4) The Secretary of State may approve for the purposes of section 16(9) above any scheme that appears to him to secure the provision of adequate insurance cover in relation to any certificate that is given under paragraph (a) of that subsection and is a certificate to which the scheme applies.

(5) Building regulations may prescribe for the purposes of section 16(9) above the insurance cover that is to be provided in relation to any certificate that is given under paragraph (a) of that subsection and is not a certificate to which an approved scheme applies and may, in particular, prescribe the form and content of policies of insurance.

(6) Building regulations may—

(a) contain provision prescribing the period for which, subject to any provision made by virtue of paragraph (b) or (c) below, any such approval as is referred to in subsection (1) above continues in force,

(b) contain provision precluding the giving of, or requiring the withdrawal of, any such approval as is referred to in subsection (1) above in such circumstances as may be prescribed,

(c) contain provision authorising the withdrawal of any such approval or designation as is referred to in subsection (1) above,

(d) provide for the maintenance by the Secretary of State of a list of bodies that are for the time being designated by him as mentioned in subsection (1) above and for the maintenance by the Secretary of State and by each designated body of a list of persons for the time being approved by him or them as mentioned in that subsection,

(e) make provision for the supply to local authorities of copies of any list of approved persons maintained by virtue of paragraph (d) above and for such copy lists to be made available for inspection, and

(f) make provision for the supply, on payment of a prescribed fee, of a certified copy of any entry in a list maintained by virtue of paragraph (d) above or in a copy list held by a local authority by virtue of paragraph (e) above.

(7) Unless the contrary is proved, in any proceedings (whether civil or criminal) a document that appears to the court to be a certified copy of an entry either in a list maintained as mentioned in subsection (6)(d) above or in a copy of such a list supplied as mentioned in subsection (6)(e) above—

(a) is presumed to be a true copy of an entry in the current list so maintained, and

(b) is evidence of the matters stated in it.

18 Building over sewer etc.

(1) Where—

(a) plans of a building or of an extension of a building are, in accordance with building regulations, deposited with a local authority, and

(b) it is proposed to erect the building or extension, as the case may be, over a sewer or drain that is shown on the relative map of sewers,

the authority shall reject the plans unless they are satisfied that in the circumstances of the particular case they may properly consent to the erection of the proposed building or extension, either unconditionally or subject to compliance with any requirements specified in their consent.

(2) Where—

(a) plans of a building or of an extension of a building are, in accordance with building regulations, deposited with the council of a district or outer London borough, or a building notice in respect of a building or of an extension of a building is served on the district surveyor in pursuance of section 83 of the London Building Acts (Amendment) Act 1939, and

(b) it is proposed to erect the building or extension, as the case may be, over a water authority's sewer that is shown on the relative map of sewers,

the council of the district or borough or the Greater London Council, as the case may be, shall notify the water authority of the proposal.

(3) A water authority may give directions to the council of a district or outer London borough as to the manner in which the council are to exercise their functions under subsection (1) above.

(4) Any question arising under subsection (1) above between a local authority and the person by whom or on whose behalf plans are deposited as to—

(a) whether the site on which it is proposed to erect a building or an extension of a building is over such a sewer or drain as is mentioned in that subsection, or

(b) whether, and if so upon what conditions, a consent ought to be given by the local authority, may on the application of that person be determined by a magistrates' court.

(5) In this section—

" drain " includes a pipe (including associated works) provided in pursuance of section 12(6), 14(5), 21(4) or 26 of the Control of Pollution Act 1974 ;

" map of sewers " means—

(a) the map/of sewers and drains kept by an authority under section 32(1) of the Public Health Act 1936, or

(b) a map of pipes kept by an authority under section 28(1) of the Control of Pollution Act 1974.

19 Use of short-lived materials

(1) Where plans of a building are, in accordance with building regulations, deposited with a local authority, and the plans show that it is proposed to construct a building of materials to which this section applies, or to place or assemble Ion the site a building constructed of such materials, the authority may, notwithstanding that the plans conform with the regulations—

(a) reject the plans, or

(b) in passing the plans—

(i) fix a period on the expiration of which the building must be removed, and

(ii) impose with respect to the use of the building such reasonable conditions, if any, as having regard to the nature of the materials used in its construction they deem appropriate,

but no condition shall be imposed that conflicts with any condition imposed on the grant of planning permission for that building under Part III of the Town and Country Planning Act 1971.

(2) If a building in respect of which plans ought under the building regulations to have been deposited, but have not been deposited, appears to the authority to be constructed of such materials as aforesaid, the authority, without prejudice to their right to take proceedings in respect of any contravention of the regulations, may—

(a) fix a period on the expiration of which the building must be removed, and

(b) if they think fit, impose such conditions with respect to the use of the building as might have been imposed under subsection (1) above upon the passing of plans for the building,

and where they fix such a period they shall forthwith give notice thereof, and of any conditions imposed, to the owner of the building.

(3) A local authority may from time to time extend any period fixed, or vary any conditions imposed, under this section; but, unless an application in that behalf is made to them by the owner of the building in question, they shall not exercise their power of varying conditions except when granting an extension, or further extension, of the period fixed with respect to the building.

(4) A person aggrieved by the action of a local authority under this section in rejecting plans, or in fixing or refusing to extend any period, or in imposing or refusing to vary any conditions, may appeal to a magistrates' court.

(5) The owner of a building in respect of which a period has been fixed under this section shall, on the expiration of that period, or, as the case may be, of that period as extended, remove the building, and, if he fails to do so—

(a) the local authority shall remove it and may recover from him the expenses reasonably incurred by them in so doing, and

(b) without prejudice to the right of the authority to exercise that power, he is liable on summary conviction to a fine not exceeding level 1 on the standard scale and to a further fine not exceeding £5 for each day during which the building is allowed to remain after he is convicted.

(6) A person who uses a building in contravention of a condition imposed under this section, or who permits a building to be so used, is liable on summary conviction to a fine not exceeding level 1 on the standard scale and to a further fine not exceeding £5 for each day on which the offence continues after he is convicted.

(7) Building regulations may provide that this section applies to any materials specified in the regulations as being materials that are, in the absence of special care, liable to rapid deterioration, or are otherwise unsuitable for use in the construction of permanent buildings.

(8) This section applies in relation to an extension of an existing building as it applies in relation to a new building.

(9) This section ceases to have effect upon the coming into force of section 20 below (which supersedes it).

20 Use of materials unsuitable for permanent building

(1) Where plans of any proposed work are, in accordance with building regulations, deposited with a local authority, and the plans show that the proposed work would include or consist of work to which this section applies, the authority may, notwithstanding that the plans conform with the regulations—

(a) reject the plans, or

(b) in passing the plans—

(i) fix a period on the expiration of which the work to which this section applies or the relevant building (as the authority may in passing the plans direct) must be removed, and

(ii) if they think fit, impose with respect to the use of the relevant building or with respect to the work to which this section applies such reasonable conditions, if any, as they consider appropriate,

but no condition as to the use of the relevant building shall be imposed that conflicts with any condition imposed or having effect as if imposed under Part III or IV of the Town and Country Planning Act 1971.

(2) If, in the case of any work in respect of which plans ought by virtue of building regulations to have been deposited with a local authority but have not been so deposited, the work appears to the authority to include or consist of work to which this section applies, the authority, without prejudice to their right to take proceedings in respect of any contravention of the regulations, may—

(a) fix a period on the expiration of which the work to which this section applies or the relevant building (as the authority may in fixing the period direct) must be removed, and

(b) if they think fit, impose any conditions that might have been imposed under subsection (1) above in passing plans for the first-mentioned work,

and where they fix such a period they shall forthwith give notice thereof, and of any conditions imposed, to the owner of the relevant building.

(3) If, in the case of any work appearing to the local authority to fall within subsection (9)(b) below, plans of the work were not required by building regulations to be deposited with the authority, and were not so deposited, the authority may at any time within 12 months from the date of completion of the work—

(a) fix a period on the expiration of which the work must be removed, and

(b) if they think fit, impose any conditions that, if plans of the work had been required to be, and had been, so deposited, might have been imposed under subsection (1) above in passing the plans,

and where they fix such a period they shall forthwith give notice thereof, and of any conditions imposed, to the owner of the relevant building.

(4) A local authority may from time to time extend any period fixed, or vary any conditions imposed, under this section, but, unless an application in that behalf is made to them by the owner of the relevant building, they shall not exercise their power of varying conditions so imposed except when granting an extension or further extension of the period fixed with respect to the work or building, as the case may be.

(5) A person aggrieved by the action of a local authority under this section—

(a) in rejecting plans,

(b) in fixing or refusing to extend any period, or

(c) in imposing or refusing to vary any conditions,

may appeal to the Secretary of State within the prescribed time and in the prescribed manner.

(6) Where a period has been fixed under this section with respect to any work to which this section applies or with respect to the relevant building—

(a) the owner of that building shall on the expiration of that period, or, as the case may be, of that period as extended, remove the work or building with respect to which the period was fixed, and

(b) if he fails to do so, the local authority may remove that work or building, as the case may be, and may recover from him the expenses reasonably incurred by them in doing so.

(7) A person who—

(a) contravenes a condition imposed under this section or permits such a condition to be contravened, or

(b) contravenes subsection (6) above,

is liable on summary conviction to a fine not exceeding level 5 on the standard scale and to a further fine not exceeding £50 for each day on which the offence continues or, as the case may be, on which the work or building is allowed to remain after he is convicted ; but this subsection does not prejudice a local authority's rights under subsection (6) above.

(8) In this section, "the relevant building" means, in any particular case, the building mentioned in paragraph (a) or, as the case may be, paragraph (b) of subsection (9) below.

(9) This section applies to—

(a) any work consisting of a part of a building, being a part in the construction of which there is used any material or component of a type that, in relation to a part of that description, is prescribed for the purposes of this paragraph under subsection (10) below, and

(b) any work provided in or in connection with a building, being work consisting of a service, fitting or item of equipment of a type so prescribed for the purposes of this paragraph.

(10) The Secretary of State may by building regulations—

(a) prescribe a type of material or component for the purposes of subsection (9)(a) above if in his opinion materials or components of that type are likely to be unsuitable for use in the construction of a particular part of a permanent building in the absence of conditions with respect to the use of the building or with respect to any material or component of that type used in the construction of a part of that description,

(b) prescribe a type of service, fitting or equipment for the purposes of subsection (9)(b) above if in his opinion services, fittings or equipment of that type are likely to be unsuitable for provision in or in connection with a permanent building in the absence of conditions with respect to the use of the building or with respect to a service, fitting or equipment of that type so provided.

(11) Upon section 19 above ceasing to have effect—

(a) any building regulations made, period fixed, condition imposed or other thing done by virtue of the said section 19 shall be deemed to have been made, fixed, imposed or done by virtue of this section, and

(b) anything begun under the said section 19 may be continued under this Act as if begun under this section, but any appeal under section 19(4) that is pending at the time when the said section 19 ceases to have effect, and any proceedings arising out of such an appeal, shall proceed as if that section were still in force.

21 Provision of drainage

(1) Where plans of a building or of an extension of a building are, in accordance with building regulations, deposited with a local authority, the authority shall reject the plans unless—

(a) the plans show that satisfactory provision will be made for the drainage of the building or of the extension, as the case may be, or

(b) the authority are satisfied that in the case of the particular building or extension they may properly dispense with any provision for drainage.

(2) In subsection (1) above, " drainage " includes the conveyance, by means of a sink and any other necessary appliance, of refuse water and the conveyance of rain-water from roofs.

(3) Any question arising under subsection (1) above between a local authority and the person by whom, or on whose behalf, plans are deposited as to—

(a) whether provision for drainage may properly be dispensed with, or

(b) whether any provision for drainage proposed to be made ought to be accepted by the authority as satisfactory,

may on the application of that person be determined by a magistrates' court.

(4) A proposed drain shall not be deemed a satisfactory drain for the purposes of this section unless it is proposed to be made, as the local authority, or on appeal a magistrates' court, may require, either to connect with a sewer, or to discharge into a cesspool or some other place; but a drain shall not be required to be made to connect with a sewer unless—

(a) that sewer is within one hundred feet of the site of the building or, in the case of an extension, the site either of the extension or of the original building, and is at a level that makes it reasonably practicable to construct a drain to communicate with it, and, if it is not a public sewer, is a sewer that the person constructing the drain is entitled to use, and

(b) the intervening land is land through which that person is entitled to construct a drain.

(5) Notwithstanding paragraph (a) of subsection (4) above, a drain may be required to be made to connect with a sewer that is not within the distance mentioned in that paragraph, but is otherwise such a sewer as is therein mentioned, if the authority undertake to bear so much of the expenses reasonably incurred in constructing, and in maintaining and repairing, the drain as may be attributable to the fact that the distance of the sewer exceeds the distance so mentioned.

(6) If any question arises as to the amount of a payment to be made to a person under subsection (5) above, that question may on his application be determined by a magistrates' court, or he may require it to be referred to arbitration.

22 Drainage of buildings in combination

(1) Where—

(a) a local authority might under section 21 above require each of two or more buildings to be drained separately into an existing sewer, but

(b) it appears to the authority that those buildings may be drained more economically or advantageously in combination,

the authority may, when the drains of the buildings are first laid, require that the buildings be drained in combination into the existing sewer by means of a private sewer to be constructed either by the owners of the buildings in such manner as the authority may direct or, if the authority so elect, by the authority on behalf of the owners.

(2) A local authority shall not, except by agreement with the owners concerned, exercise the power conferred by subsection (1) above in respect of any building for whose drainage plans have been previously passed by them.

(3) A local authority who make such a requirement as aforesaid shall fix—

(a) the proportions in which the expenses of constructing, and of maintaining and repairing, the private sewer are to be borne by the owners concerned, or

(b) in a case in which the distance of the existing sewer from the site of any of the buildings in question is or exceeds one hundred feet, the proportions in which those expenses are to borne by the owners concerned and the local authority,

and shall forthwith give notice of their decision to each owner affected.

(4) An owner aggrieved by the decision of a local authority under subsection (3) above may appeal to a magistrates' court

(5) Subject to any such appeal—

(a) any expenses reasonably incurred in constructing, or in maintaining or repairing, the private sewer shall be borne in the proportions so fixed, and

(b) those expenses, or, as the case may be, contributions to them, may be recovered accordingly by the persons, whether the local authority or the owners, by whom they were incurred in the first instance.

(6) A sewer constructed by a local authority under this section is not deemed a public sewer by reason of the fact that the expenses of its construction are in the first instance defrayed by the authority, or that some part of those expenses is borne by them.

23 Provision of facilities for refuse

(1) Where plans for the erection or extension of a building are, in accordance with building regulations, deposited with a local authority, the local authority shall reject the plans unless it is shown to them that satisfactory means of access from the building to a street for the purpose of the removal of refuse, and satisfactory means of storing refuse for removal, can, and will, be provided.

(2) Any question arising under subsection (1) above between a local authority and the person by whom, or on whose behalf, plans are deposited as to whether a means of access or of storing refuse proposed to be provided can be provided and ought to be accepted by the authority as satisfactory may on the application of that person be determined by a magistrates' court.

(3) It is unlawful for any person except with the consent of the local authority to close or obstruct the means of access by which refuse or faecal matter is removed from a building, and the local authority in giving their consent may impose such conditions as they think fit with respect to the improvement of an alternative means of access or the substitution of other means of access.

(4) A person who contravenes subsection (3) above is liable on summary conviction to a fine not exceeding level 4 on the standard scale.

24 Provision of exits etc.

(1) Where—

(a) plans of a building or of an extension of a building are, in accordance with building regulations, deposited with a local authority, and

(b) the building or, as the case may be, the building as extended will be a building to which this section applies,

the authority shall reject the plans unless they show that the building, or, as the case may be, the building as extended, will be provided with such means of ingress and egress and passages or gangways as the authority, after consultation with the fire authority, deem satisfactory, regard being had to the purposes for which the building is intended to be, or is, used and the number of persons likely to resort to it at any one time.

(2) Any question arising under subsection (1) above between a local authority and the person by whom, or on whose behalf, plans are deposited as to whether the means of ingress or egress or passages or gangways already existing, or proposed to be provided, ought to be accepted by the authority as satisfactory may on the application of that person be determined by a magistrates' court.

(3) Where building regulations imposing requirements as to the provision of means of escape in case of fire are applicable to a proposed building or proposed extension of a building, or would be so applicable but for a direction under section 8 above dispensing with such requirements—

(a) this section, and

(b) any provision of a local Act that has effect in place of this section,

does not apply in relation to the proposed building or extension.

(4) Subject to subsection (3) above, this section applies to—

(a) a theatre, and a hall or other building that is used as a place of public resort,

(b) a restaurant, shop, store-or warehouse to which members of the public are admitted and in which more than twenty persons are employed,

(c) a club required to be registered under the Licensing Act 1964,

(d) a school not exempted from the operation of building regulations, and

(e) a church, chapel or other place of public worship,

but not—

(i) a private house to which members of the public are admitted occasionally or exceptionally,

(ii) a building that was used as a church, chapel or other place of public worship immediately before the date on which section 36 of the Public Health Acts Amendment Act 1890, or a corresponding provision in a local Act, came into operation in the district or rating district, or

(iii) a building that was so used immediately before the 1st October 1937 (the date of commencement of the Public Health Act 1936) in a district or rating district where neither the said section 36 nor such a corresponding provision ever came into operation.

25 Provision of water supply

(1) Where plans of a house are, in accordance with building regulations, deposited with a local authority, the authority shall reject the plans unless a proposal is put before them that appears to them to be satisfactory for providing the occupants of the house with a supply of wholesome water sufficient for their domestic purposes—

(a) by connecting the house to a supply of water in pipes provided by statutory water undertakers,

(b) if in all the circumstances it is not reasonable to require the house to be connected as aforesaid, by otherwise taking water into the house by means of a pipe, or

(c) if in all the circumstances neither of the preceding alternatives can reasonably be required, by providing a supply of water within a reasonable distance of the house,

and the authority are satisfied that the proposal can and will be carried into effect.

(2) Any question arising under subsection (1) above between a local authority and the person by whom, or on whose behalf, plans are deposited as to whether the local authority ought to pass the plans may on the application of that person be determined by a magistrates' court.

(3) If, after any such plans as aforesaid have been passed, it appears to the local authority that the proposal for providing a supply of water—

(a) has not been carried into effect, or

(b) has not resulted in a supply of wholesome water sufficient for the domestic purposes of the occupants,

the authority shall give notice to the owner of the house prohibiting him from occupying it, or permitting it to be occupied, until the authority, being satisfied that such a supply has been provided, have granted him a certificate to that effect.

(4) Until a certificate is granted under subsection (3) above, the owner shall not occupy the house or permit it to be occupied.

(5) A person aggrieved by the refusal of the authority to grant such a certificate may apply to a magistrates' court for an order authorising the occupation of the house, and, if the court is of opinion that a certificate ought to have been granted, the court may make an order authorising the occupation of the house, and such an order shall have the like effect as a certificate of the local authority.

(6) A person who contravenes subsection (4) above is liable on summary conviction to a fine not exceeding level 1 on the standard scale and to a further fine not exceeding £2 for each day on which the offence continues after he is convicted.

26 Provision of closets

(1) Where plans of a building or of an extension of a building are, in accordance with building regulations, deposited with a local authority, the authority shall reject the plans unless—

(a) the plans show that sufficient and satisfactory closet accommodation consisting of one or more water-closets or earth-closets, as the authority may approve, will be provided, or

(b) the authority are satisfied that in the case of the particular building or extension they may properly dispense with the provision of closet accommodation.

(2) Notwithstanding subsection (1) above—

(a) the authority shall not reject the plans on the ground that the proposed accommodation consists of or includes an earth-closet or earth-closets unless a sufficient water supply and sewer are available, and

(b) the authority shall reject the plans if they show that the proposed building or, as the case may be, extension is likely to be used as a factory or workplace in which persons of both sexes will be employed or will be in attendance, unless—

(i) the plans show that sufficient and satisfactory separate closet accommodation for persons of each sex will be provided, or

(ii) the authority are satisfied that in the circumstances of the particular case they may properly dispense with the provision of such separate accommodation.

(3) Any question arising under subsection (1) or (2) above between a local authority and the person by whom, or on whose behalf, plans are deposited as to—

(a) whether the provision of closet accommodation or, as the case may be, the provision of separate closet accommodation for persons of each sex may properly be dispensed with,

(b) whether the closet accommodation proposed to be provided is sufficient and satisfactory or, as the case may be, sufficient and satisfactory for persons of either sex, or

(c) whether the provision of an earth-closet in lieu of a water-closet should in a particular instance be approved,

may on the application of that person be determined by a magistrates' court.

27 Provision of bathrooms

(1) Where plans—

(a) for the erection of a house, or of a building part of which is intended to be occupied as a separate dwelling, or

(b) of works involving the conversion of a building into a house or into separate dwellings, or the conversion of part of a building into a separate dwelling,

are, in accordance with building regulations, deposited with a local authority, the authority may reject the plans if they do not show that the house or, as the case may be, each separate dwelling will be provided with a bathroom containing either a fixed bath or a shower bath, and a suitable installation for the provision of hot and cold water to the bath or shower bath.

(2) If the local authority reject the plans under subsection (1) above, the person by whom the plans were deposited may appeal to a magistrates' court, and if the magistrates' court allows the appeal it shall direct the local authority to allow the plans under this section.

28 Provision for food storage

(1) Where plans—

(a) for the erection of a house, or of a building part of which is intended to be occupied as a separate dwelling, or

(b) of works involving the conversion of a building into a house or into separate dwellings, or the conversion of part of a building into a separate dwelling,

are, in accordance with building regulations, deposited with a local authority, the authority may reject the plans if they do not show that the house or, as the case may be, each separate dwelling will be provided with sufficient and suitable accommodation for the storage of food, or sufficient and suitable space for the provision of such accommodation by the occupier.

(2) If the local authority reject the plans under subsection (1) above, the person by whom the plans were deposited may appeal to a magistrates' court, and if the magistrates' court allows the appeal it shall direct the local authority to allow the plans under this section.

29 Site containing offensive material

(1) Where plans for the erection or extension of a building are, in accordance with building regulations, deposited with a local authority, and the site on which it is proposed to erect the building or the extension, as the case may be, is—

(a) ground that has been filled up with material impregnated with faecal or offensive animal or offensive vegetable matter, or

(b) ground upon which any such material has been deposited,

the authority shall reject the plans unless they are satisfied that the material in question has been removed, or has become or been rendered innocuous.

(2) Any question arising under subsection (1) above between a local authority and the person by whom or on whose behalf plans are deposited as to whether the local authority ought to approve the erection of the building or the extension, as the case may be, on the site in question may on the application of that person be determined by a magistrates' court.

Determination of questions

30 Determination of questions

(1) If any question arises between a local authority and a person who has executed, or proposes to execute, any work—

(a) as to the application to that work of any building regulations,

(b) whether the plans of the work are in conformity with building regulations, or

(c) whether the work has been executed in accordance with the plans as passed by the authority,

the question may, on an application made jointly by him and the local authority, be referred to the Secretary of State for determination, and his decision is final.

(2) The Secretary of State may at any stage of the proceedings on the reference, and shall if so directed by the High Court, state in the form of a special case for the opinion of the High Court any question of law arising in those proceedings.

(3) The Secretary of State may by order repeal the words ", and his decision is final" in subsection (1) above.

(4) The Secretary of State may by order repeal this section, but such a repeal does not affect applications referred to him before the date on which the repeal takes effect.

Proposed departure from plans

31 Proposed departure from plans

(1) Where plans of any proposed work have been passed under section 16 above by a local authority, the person by or on whose behalf the plans were in accordance with building regulations deposited with the authority may, and in such cases as may be prescribed shall, for the purpose of obtaining the approval of the authority to any proposed departure or deviation from the plans as passed, deposit plans of the departure or deviation.

(2) Section 16 above applies in relation to plans deposited under subsection (1) above as it applies in relation to the plans originally deposited.

Lapse of deposit of plans

32 Lapse of deposit of plans

(1) Where plans of any proposed work have, in accordance with building regulations, been deposited with a local authority, and—

(a) the plans have been passed by the authority, or

(b) notice of rejection of the plans has not been given with in the relevant period from their deposit,

and the work to which the plans relate has not been commenced within three years from the deposit of the plans, the local authority may, at any time before the work is commenced, by notice to the person by whom or on whose behalf the plans were deposited, or other the owner for the time being of the land to which the plans relate, declare that the deposit of the plans is of no effect.

(2) Where a notice has been given under subsection (1) above, this Act and the building regulations shall, as respects the proposed work, have effect as if no plans had been deposited.

Tests for conformity with building regulations

33 Tests for conformity with building regulations

(1) The following subsection has effect for the purpose of enabling a local authority to ascertain, as regards any work or proposed work to which building regulations for the enforcement of which they are responsible are applicable, whether any provision of building regulations is or would be contravened by, or by anything done or proposed to be done in connection with, that work.

(2) The local authority have power for that purpose—

(a) to require a person by whom or on whose behalf the work was, is being or is proposed to be done to carry out such reasonable tests of or in connection with the work as may be specified in the requirement, or

(b) themselves to carry out any reasonable tests of or in connection with the work, and to take any samples necessary to enable them to carry out such a test.

(3) Without prejudice to the generality of subsection (2) above, the matters with respect to which tests may be required or carried out under that subsection includes—

(a) tests of the soil or subsoil of the site of a building,

(b) tests of any material, component or combination of components that has been, is being or is proposed to be used in the construction of a building, and tests of any service, fitting or equipment that has been, is being or is proposed to be provided in or in connection with a building.

(4) A local authority have power, for the purpose of ascertaining whether there is or has been, in the case of a building, a contravention of a continuing requirement that applies in relation to that building—

(a) to require the owner or occupier of the building to carry out such reasonable tests as may be specified in the requirement under this paragraph, or

(b) themselves to carry out any tests that they have power to require under paragraph (a) above, and to take any samples necessary to enable them to carry out such a test;

and in this subsection " continuing requirement" means a continuing requirement imposed by building regulations made by virtue of section 2(1) or (2) above.

(5) The expense of carrying out any tests that a person is required to carry out under this section shall be met by that person, except that the local authority, on an application made to them, may, if they think it reasonable to do so, direct that the expense of carrying out any such tests, or such part of that expense as may be specified in the direction, shall be met by the local authority.

(6) Any question arising under this section between a local authority and a person as to the reasonableness of—

(a) a test specified in a requirement imposed on him by the authority under this section,

(b) a refusal by the authority to give a direction under subsection (5) above on an application made by him, or

(c) a direction under that subsection given on such an application,

may on the application of that person be determined by a magistrates' court; and in a case falling within paragraph (b) or (c) above the court may order the expense to which the application relates to be met by the local authority to such extent as the court thinks just.

Classification of buildings

34 Classification of buildings

For the purposes of building regulations and of a direction given or instrument made with reference to building regulations, buildings may be classified by reference to size, description, design, purpose, location or any other characteristic whatsoever.

Breach of building regulations

35 Penalty for contravening building regulations

If a person contravenes any provision contained in building regulations, other than a provision designated in the regulations as one to which this section does not apply, he is liable on summary conviction to a fine not exceeding level 5 on the standard scale and to a further fine not exceeding £50 for each day on which the default continues after he is convicted.

36 Removal or alteration of offending work

(1) If any work to which building regulations are applicable contravenes any of those regulations, the local authority, without prejudice to their right to take proceedings for a fine in respect of the contravention, may by notice require the owner—

(a) to pull down or remove the work, or

(b) if he so elects, to effect such alterations in it as may be necessary to make it comply with the regulations.

(2) If, in a case where the local authority are, by any section of this Part of this Act other than section 16, expressly required or authorised to reject plans, any work to which building regulations are applicable is executed—

(a) without plans having been deposited,

(b) notwithstanding the rejection of the plans, or

(c) otherwise than in accordance with any requirements subject to which the authority passed the plans,

the authority may by notice to the owner—

(i) require him to pull down or remove the work, or

(ii) require him either to pull down or remove the work or, if he so elects, to comply with any other requirements specified in the notice, being requirements that they might have made under the section in question as a condition of passing plans.

(3) If a person to whom a notice has been given under subsection (1) or (2) above fails to comply with the notice before the expiration of 28 days, or such longer period as a magistrates' court may on his application allow, the local authority may—

(a) pull down or remove the work in question, or

(b) effect such alterations in it as they deem necessary,

and may recover from him the expenses reasonably incurred by them in doing so.

(4) A notice under subsection (1) or (2) above (called a " section 36 notice ") shall not be given after the expiration of 12 months from the date of the completion of the work in question.

(5) A section 36 notice shall not be given, in a case where plans were deposited and the work was shown on them, on the ground that the work contravenes any building regulations or, as the case may be, does not comply with the authority's requirements under any section of this Part of this Act other than section 16, if—

(a) the plans were passed by the authority, or

(b) notice of their rejection was not given within the relevant period from their deposit,

and if the work has been executed in accordance with the plans and of any requirement made by the local authority as a condition of passing the plans.

(6) This section does not affect the right of a local authority, the Attorney General or any other person to apply for an injunction for the removal or alteration of any work on the ground that it contravenes any regulation or any provision of this Act; but if—

(a) the work is one in respect of which plans were deposited,

(b) the plans were passed by the local authority, or notice of their rejection was not given within the relevant period from their deposit, and

(c) the work has been executed in accordance with the plans,

the court on granting an injunction has power to order the local authority to pay to the owner of the work such compensation as the court thinks just, but before making any such order the court shall in accordance with rules of court cause the local authority, if not a party to the proceedings, to be joined as a party to them.

37 Obtaining of report where section 36 notice given

(1) In a case where—

(a) a person to whom a section 36 notice has been given gives to the local authority by whom the notice was given notice of his intention to obtain from a suitably qualified person a written report concerning work to which the section 36 notice relates, and

(b) such a report is obtained and submitted to the local authority and, as a result of their consideration of it, the local authority withdraw the section 36 notice,

the local authority may pay to the person to whom the section 36 notice was given such amount as appears to them to represent the expenses reasonably incurred by him in consequence of their having given him that notice including, in particular, his expenses in obtaining the report.

(2) Subject to subsection (3) below, if a person to whom a section 36 notice has been given gives notice under subsection (1)(a) above, then, so far as regards the matters to which the section 36 notice relates, the reference to 28 days in section 36(3) above shall be construed as a reference to 70 days.

(3) Notice under subsection (1)(a) above shall be given before the expiry of the period of 28 days referred to in section 36(3) above, or, as the case may be, within such longer period as a court allows under section 36(3); and, where such a longer period has been so allowed before notice is given under subsection (1)(a) above, subsection (2) above does not apply.

38 Civil liability

(1) Subject to this section—

(a) breach of a duty imposed by building regulations, so far as it causes damage, is actionable, except in so far as the regulations provide otherwise, and

(b) as regards such a duty, building regulations may provide for a prescribed defence to be available in an action for breach of that duty brought by virtue of this subsection.

(2) Subsection (1) above, and any defence provided for in regulations made by virtue of it, do not apply in the case of a breach of such a duty in connection with a building erected before the date on which that subsection comes into force unless the regulations imposing the duty apply to or in connection with the building by virtue of section 2(2) above or paragraph 8 of Schedule 1 to this Act

(3) This section does not affect the extent (if any) to which breach of—

(a) a duty imposed by or arising in connection with this Part of this Act or any other enactment relating to building regulations, or

(b) a duty imposed by building regulations in a case to which subsection (1) above does not apply,

is actionable, or prejudice a right of action that exists apart from the enactments relating to building regulations.

(4) In this section, " damage" includes the death of, or injury to, any person (including any disease and any impairment of a person's physical or mental condition).

Appeals in certain cases

39 Appeal against refusal etc. to relax building regulations

(1) If a local authority refuse an application to dispense with or relax a requirement in building regulations that they have power to dispense with or relax, the applicant may by notice in writing appeal to the Secretary of State within one month from the date on which the local authority notify the applicant of their refusal.

(2) If, within—

(a) a period of two months beginning with the date of an application, or

(b) such extended period as may at any time be agreed in writing between the applicant and the local authority,

the local authority do not notify the applicant of their decision on the application, subsection (1) above applies in relation to the application as if the local authority had refused the application and notified the applicant of their decision at the end of the said period.

(3) The notice of appeal shall set out the grounds of appeal, and a copy of the notice of appeal shall be sent to the local authority.

(4) The local authority, on receiving a copy of the notice of appeal, shall at once transmit to the Secretary of State a copy of the application and a copy of all the documents furnished by the applicant for the purposes of his application.

(5) The local authority shall at the same time give to the Secretary of State in writing any representations that they desire to make as regards the appeal, and shall send a copy to the appellant.

(6) If the Secretary of State allows the appeal, he shall give such directions for dispensing with or relaxing building regulations as may be appropriate.

40 Appeal against section 36 notice

(1) A person aggrieved by the giving of a section 36 notice may appeal to a magistrates' court acting for the petty sessions area in which is situated land on which there has been carried out any work to which the notice relates.

(2) Subject to subsection (3) below, on an appeal under this section the court shall—

(a) if it determines that the local authority were entitled to give the notice, confirm the notice, and

(b) in any other case, give the local authority a direction to withdraw the notice.

(3) If, in a case where the appeal is against a notice under section 36(2) above, the court is satisfied that—

(a) the local authority were entitled to give the notice, but
(b) in all the circumstances of the case the purpose for which was enacted the section of this Act by virtue of which the notice was given has been substantially achieved,

the court may give a direction under subsection (2)(b) above.

(4) An appeal under this section shall be brought—
(a) within 28 days of the giving of the section 36 notice, or
(b) in a case where the person to whom the section 36 notice was given gives notice under section 37(1)(a) above, within 70 days of the giving of the section 36 notice.

(5) Where an appeal is brought under this section—
(a) the section 36 notice is of no effect pending the final determination or withdrawal of the appeal, and
(b) section 36(3) above has effect in relation to that notice as if after the words " 28 days " there were inserted the words " (beginning, in a case where an appeal is brought under section 40 below, on the date when the appeal is finally determined or, as the case may be, withdrawn) " .

(6) If, on an appeal under this section, there is produced to the court a report that has been submitted to the local authority under section 37(1) above, the court, in making an order as to costs, may treat the expenses incurred in obtaining the report as expenses incurred for the purposes of the appeal.

41 Appeal to Crown Court

(1) Where a person—
(a) is aggrieved by an order, determination or other decision of a magistrates' court under this Part of this Act, or under Part IV of this Act as it applies in relation to this Part, and
(b) is not by any other enactment authorised to appeal to the Crown Court,

he may appeal to the Crown Court.

(2) Subsection (1) above does not confer a right of appeal in a case in which each of the parties concerned might under this Act have required that the dispute should be determined by arbitration instead of by a magistrates' court.

42 Appeal and statement of case to High Court in certain cases

(1) Where the Secretary of State gives a decision in proceedings—
(a) on an appeal under section 20 or 39 above,
(b) on a reference under section 16 above or 50 below, or
(c) on an application for a direction under section 8 above where the power of giving the direction is not exercisable by the local authority,

the relevant person or the local authority or, as the case may be, the approved inspector may appeal to the High Court against the decision on a point of law.

(2) In subsection (1) above, " the relevant person " means—
(a) as regards an appeal under the said section 20 or 39, the appellant,

(b) as regards a reference under the said section 16 or 50, the person on whose application the reference was made,

(c) as regards such an application as is mentioned in subsection (1)(c) above, the applicant.

(3) At any stage of the proceedings on such an appeal, reference or application as is mentioned in subsection (1) above—

(a) the Secretary of State may state a question of law arising in the course of the proceedings in the form of a special case for the decision of the High Court, and

(b) a decision of the High Court on a case so stated is deemed to be a judgment of the court within the meaning of section 16 of the Supreme Court Act 1981 (appeals from the High Court to the Court of Appeal).

(4) In relation to proceedings in the High Court or the Court of Appeal brought by virtue of this section, the power to make rules of court includes power to make rules—

(a) prescribing the powers of the High Court or the Court of Appeal with respect to the remitting of the matter with the opinion or direction of the court for re-hearing and determination by the Secretary of State, and

(b) providing for the Secretary of State, either generally or in such circumstances as may be prescribed by the rules, to be treated as a party to any such proceedings and to be entitled to appear and to be heard accordingly.

(5) No appeal to the Court of Appeal shall be brought by virtue of this section except with the leave of the High Court or the Court of Appeal.

(6) In this section, " decision " includes a direction, and references to the giving of a decision shall be construed accordingly.

(7) Until such day as the Secretary of State may by order appoint, subsections (1) and (2) above have effect as if—

(a) in subsection (1)(b), for " section 16 above or 50 below " there were substituted " section 30 above " ,

(b) in subsection (1), the words " or, as the case may be, the approved inspector " were omitted, and

(c) in subsection (2)(b), for " section 16 or 50 " there were substituted " section 30 " and the words " (jointly with the local authority) " were inserted after " application "

43 Procedure on appeal to Secretary of State on certain matters

(1) On an appeal to the Secretary of State under section 20 or 39 above, the Secretary of State may at his discretion afford to the appellant and the local authority an opportunity of appearing before, and being heard by, a person appointed by the Secretary of State for the purpose.

(2) On determining such an appeal, the Secretary of State shall give such directions, if any, as he considers appropriate for giving effect to his determination.

(3) Without prejudice to paragraph 10(c) of Schedule 1 to this Act, building regulations may, in connection with such an appeal, include such supplementary provisions with respect to procedure as the Secretary of State thinks fit.

Application of building regulations to Crown etc.

44 Application to Crown

(1) Except in so far as buildings regulations provide otherwise, the substantive requirements of building regulations—

(a) apply in relation to work carried out or proposed to be carried out by or on behalf of a Crown authority (whether or not in relation to a Crown building) as they would apply if the person by or on behalf of whom the work was or is to be carried out were not a Crown authority, and

(b) so far as they consist of continuing requirements, apply to Crown authorities (whether or not in relation to Crown buildings) as they apply to persons who are not Crown authorities.

(2) In so far as building regulations so provide as regards any of the substantive requirements of building regulations, those requirements—

(a) apply in relation to work carried out or proposed to be carried out as mentioned in subsection (1)(a) above in inner London, and

(b) so far as they consist of continuing requirements, apply to Crown authorities there as mentioned in subsection (1)(b) above,

even if those requirements do not apply there in the case of work carried out or proposed to be carried out otherwise than by or on behalf of a Crown authority or, in the case of continuing requirements, do not apply there to persons other than Crown authorities.

(3) Except in so far as building regulations provide otherwise, building regulations and the enactments relating to building regulations—

(a) apply in relation to work carried out or proposed to be carried out in relation to a Crown building otherwise than by or on behalf of a Crown authority, and, in the case of section 2 above and building regulations made by virtue of it, apply in relation to a Crown building to persons other than Crown authorities, as they would apply if the building were not a Crown building, and

(b) apply in relation to work carried out or proposed to be carried out by or on behalf of a government department acting for a person other than a Crown authority as they would apply if the work had been or were to be carried out by that person.

(4) Section 38 above and any building regulations made by virtue of subsection (1) of that section apply in relation to duties imposed by building regulations in their application in accordance with subsections (1) to (3) above.

(5) Where—

(a) work is carried out or proposed to be carried out by or on behalf of a Crown authority, or

(b) a Crown authority is or (apart from any dispensation or relaxation) will be subject to continuing requirements,

that authority may exercise the like powers of dispensing with or relaxing the substantive requirements of building regulations or, as the case may be, the continuing requirements in question as are conferred on the Secretary of State and local authorities by virtue of section 8 above (other than a power that by virtue of paragraph 6 of Schedule 1 to this Act is exercisable otherwise than by a local authority), subject to—

(i) the like requirements as to consultation (if any) as apply by virtue of paragraph 3 of Schedule 1 to this Act in the case of a local authority (but not the requirements of the said section 8 as to consultation with the local authority), and

(ii) the like requirements as in the case of the Secretary of State apply by virtue of section 10 above,

and no application is necessary for the exercise of any such powers by virtue of this subsection.

(6) In relation to continuing requirements, references in subsection (5) above to section 8 above are references to it as modified by section 2(6) above.

(7) For the purposes of subsection (5) above, work carried out or proposed to be carried out by or on behalf of a government department acting for another Crown authority shall be treated as carried out or proposed to be carried out by or on behalf of that department (and not by or on behalf of the other Crown authority).

(8) In this section—

" continuing requirement" means a continuing requirement of building regulations imposed by virtue of section 2(1) or (2)(a) or (b) above;

" Crown authority" means the Crown Estate Commissioners, a Minister of the Crown, a government department, any other person or body whose functions are performed on behalf of the Crown (not being a person or body whose functions are performed on behalf of Her Majesty in her private capacity), or a person acting in right of the Duchy of Lancaster or the Duchy of Cornwall;

" Crown building " means a building in which there is a Crown interest or a Duchy interest;

" Crown interest" means an interest belonging to Her Majesty in right of the Crown, or belonging to a government department, or held in trust for Her Majesty for the purposes of a government department;

" Duchy interest" means an interest belonging to Her Majesty in right of the Duchy of Lancaster, or belonging to the Duchy of Cornwall.

(9) If any question arises under this section as to which Crown authority is entitled to exercise any such powers as are mentioned in subsection (5) above, that question shall be referred to the Treasury, whose decision is final.

(10) This section, with any necessary modifications, applies in relation to the making of a material change in the use of a building within the meaning of building regulations made for the purposes of paragraph 8(1)(e) of Schedule 1 to this Act as it applies in relation to the carrying out of work.

45 Application to United Kingdom Atomic Energy Authority

(1) The provisions of section 44(1) and (4) to (10) above apply in relation to the United Kingdom Atomic Energy Authority (in this section referred to as " the Authority ") as if—

(a) the Authority were a Crown authority,

(b) a building belonging to or occupied by the Authority were a Crown building, and

(c) the references in subsection (1) to not being a Crown authority were references to being neither a Crown authority nor the Authority,

but the said provisions do not by virtue of this subsection apply in relation to dwelling-houses or offices belonging to or occupied by the Authority.

(2) Subject to the said provisions as applied by subsection (1) above, building regulations and the enactments relating to building regulations do not apply in relation to buildings belonging to or occupied by the Authority, except dwelling-houses and offices.

Inner London

46 Inner London

In its application to inner London, this Part of this Act has effect subject to Part I of Schedule 3 to this Act.

PART II

SUPERVISION OF BUILDING WORK ETC. OTHERWISE THAN BY LOCAL AUTHORITIES

Supervision of plans and work by approved inspectors

47 Giving and acceptance of initial notice

(1) If—

(a) a notice in the prescribed form (called an " initial notice ") is given jointly to a local authority by a person intending to carry out work and a person who is an approved inspector in relation to that work,

(b) the initial notice is accompanied by such plans of the work as may be prescribed,

(c) the initial notice is accompanied by such evidence as may be prescribed that an approved scheme applies, or the prescribed insurance cover has been or will be provided, in relation to the work, and

(d) the initial notice is accepted by the local authority,

then, so long as the initial notice continues in force, the approved inspector by whom the notice was given shall undertake such functions as may be prescribed with respect to the inspection of plans of the work specified in the notice, the supervision of that work and the giving of certificates and other notices.

(2) A local authority to whom an initial notice is given—

(a) may not reject the notice except on prescribed grounds, and

(b) shall reject the notice if any of the prescribed grounds exists,

and, in a case where the work to which an initial notice relates is work of such a description that, if plans of it had been deposited with the local authority, the authority could, under any enactment, have imposed requirements as a condition of passing the plans, the local authority may impose the like requirements as a condition of accepting the initial notice.

(3) Unless, within the prescribed period, the local authority to whom an initial notice is given give notice of rejection, specifying the ground or grounds in question, to each

of the persons by whom the initial notice was given, the authority is conclusively presumed to have accepted the initial notice and to have done so without imposing any such requirements as are referred to in subsection (2) above.

(4) An initial notice—

(a) comes into force when it is accepted by the local authority, either by notice given within the prescribed period to each of the persons by whom it was given or by virtue of subsection (3) above, and

(b) subject to section 51(3) below, continues in force until—

(i) it is cancelled by a notice under section 52 below, or

(ii) the occurrence of, or the expiry of a prescribed period of time beginning on the date of, such event as may be prescribed ;

and building regulations may empower a local authority to extend (whether before or after its expiry) any such period of time as is referred to in paragraph (ii) above.

(5) The form prescribed for an initial notice may be such as to require—

(a) either or both of the persons by whom the notice is to be given to furnish information relevant for the purposes of this Act, Part II or IV of the Public Health Act 1936 or any provision of building regulations, and

(b) the approved inspector by whom the notice is to be given to enter into undertakings with respect to his performance of any of the functions referred to in subsection (1) above.

(6) The Secretary of State may approve for the purposes of this section any scheme that appears to him to secure the provision of adequate insurance cover in relation to any work that is specified in an initial notice and is work to which the scheme applies.

(7) Building regulations may prescribe for the purposes of this section the insurance cover that is to be provided in relation to any work that is specified in an initial notice and is not work to which an approved scheme applies and may, in particular, prescribe the form and content of policies of insurance.

48 Effect of initial notice

(1) So long as an initial notice continues in force, the function of enforcing building regulations that is conferred on a local authority by section 91(2) below is not exercisable in relation to the work specified in the notice, and accordingly—

(a) a local authority may not give a notice under section 36(1) above in relation to the work so specified, and

(b) a local authority may not institute proceedings under section 35 above for a contravention of building regulations that arises out of the carrying out of the work so specified.

(2) For the purposes of the enactments specified in subsection (3) below—

(a) the giving of an initial notice accompanied by such plans as are referred to in section 47(1)(b) above shall be treated as the deposit of plans,

(b) the plans accompanying an initial notice shall be treated as the deposited plans,

(c) the acceptance or rejection of an initial notice shall be treated as the passing or, as the case may be, the rejection of plans, and

(d) the cancellation of an initial notice under section 52(5) below shall be treated as a declaration under section 32 above that the deposit of plans is of no effect.

(3) The enactments referred to in subsection (2) above are—

(a) section 36(2) above,

(b) section 36(5) above, in so far as it relates to a notice under section 36(2) above and to non-compliance with any such requirement as is referred to in that subsection,

(c) section 36(6) above, in so far as it relates to a contravention of this Act,

(d) section 18(2) above, and

(e) sections 219 to 225 of the Highways Act 1980 (the advance payments code).

(4) For the purposes of section 13 of the Fire Precautions Act 1971 (exercise of fire authority's powers where provisions of building regulations as to means of escape apply)—

(a) the acceptance by a local authority of an initial notice relating to any work shall be treated as the deposit of plans of the work with the authority in accordance with building regulations, and

(b) the references in subsections (1)(ii) and (3)(b) of that section to matters or circumstances of which particulars are not or were not required by or under the building regulations to be supplied to the local authority in connection with the deposit of plans shall be construed as a reference to matters or circumstances of which particulars would not be or, as the case may be, would not have been required to be so supplied if plans were to be or had been deposited with the authority in accordance with building regulations.

49 Approved inspectors

(1) In this Act, " approved inspector " means a person who, in accordance with building regulations, is approved for the purposes of this Part of this Act—

(a) by the Secretary of State, or

(b) by a body (corporate or unincorporated) that, in accordance with the regulations, is designated by the Secretary of State for the purpose.

(2) Any such approval as is referred to in subsection (1) above may limit the description of work in relation to which the person concerned is an approved inspector.

(3) Any such designation as is referred to in subsection (1)(b) above may limit the cases in which and the terms on which the body designated may approve a person and, in particular, may provide that any approval given by the body shall be limited as mentioned in subsection (2) above.

(4) There shall be paid on an application for any such approval as is referred to in subsection (1) above—

(a) where the application is made to the Secretary of State, such fee as may be prescribed,

(b) where the application is made to a body designated by him as mentioned in that subsection, such fee as that body may determine.

(5) Building regulations may—

(a) contain provision prescribing the period for which, subject to any provision made by virtue of paragraph (b) or (c) below, any such approval as is referred to in subsection (1) above continues in force,

(b) contain provision precluding the giving of, or requiring the withdrawal of, any such approval as is referred to in subsection (1) above in such circumstances as may be prescribed,

(c) contain provision authorising the withdrawal of any such approval or designation as is referred to in subsection (1) above,

(d) provide for the maintenance—

(i) by the Secretary of State of a list of bodies that are for the time being designated by him as mentioned in subsection (1) above, and

(ii) by the Secretary of State and by each designated body of a list of persons for the time being approved by him or them as mentioned in that subsection,

(e) make provision for the supply to local authorities of copies of any list of approved inspectors maintained by virtue of paragraph (d) above and for such copy lists to be made available for inspection, and

(f) make provision for the supply, on payment of a prescribed fee, of a certified copy of any entry in a list maintained by virtue of paragraph (d) above or in a copy list held by a local authority by virtue of paragraph (e) above.

(6) Unless the contrary is proved, in any proceedings (whether civil or criminal) a document that appears to the court to be a certified copy of an entry either in a list maintained as mentioned in subsection (5)(d) above or in a copy of such a list supplied as mentioned in subsection (5)(e) above—

(a) is presumed to be a true copy of an entry in the current list so maintained, and

(b) is evidence of the matters stated in it.

(7) An approved inspector may make such charges in respect of the carrying out of the functions referred to in section 47(1) above as may in any particular case be agreed between him and the person who intends to carry out the work in question or, as the case may be, by whom that work is being or has been carried out,

(8) Nothing in this Part of this Act prevents an approved inspector from arranging for plans or work to be inspected on his behalf by another person ; but such a delegation—

(a) shall not extend to the giving of a certificate under section 50 or 51 below, and

(b) shall not affect any liability, whether civil or criminal, of the approved inspector which arises out of functions conferred on him by this Part of this Act or by building regulations,

and, without prejudice to the generality of paragraph (b) above, an approved inspector is liable for negligence on the part of a person carrying out an inspection on his behalf in like manner as if it were negligence by a servant of his acting in the course of his employment.

50 Plans certificates

(1) Where an approved inspector—

(a) has inspected plans of the work specified in an initial notice given by him,

(b) is satisfied that the plans neither are defective nor show that work carried out in accordance with them would contravene any provision of building regulations, and

(c) has complied with any prescribed requirements as to consultation or otherwise, he shall, if requested to do so by the person intending to carry out the work, give a certificate in the prescribed form (called a " plans certificate ") to the local authority and to that person.

(2) If any question arises under subsection (1) above between an approved inspector and a person who proposes to carry out any work whether plans of the work are in conformity with building regulations, that person may refer the question to the Secretary of State for his determination.

(3) An application for a reference under subsection (2) above shall be accompanied by such fee as may be prescribed.

(4) Building regulations may authorise the giving of an initial notice combined with a certificate under subsection (1) above, and may prescribe a single form for such a combined notice and certificate ; and where such a prescribed form is used—

(a) a reference in this Part of this Act to an initial notice or to a plans certificate includes a reference to that form, but

(b) should the form cease to be in force as an initial notice by virtue of section 47(4) above, nothing in that subsection affects the continuing validity of the form as a plans certificate.

(5) A plans certificate—

(a) may relate either to the whole or to part only of the work specified in the initial notice concerned, and

(b) does not have effect unless it is accepted by the local authority to whom it is given.

(6) A local authority to whom a plans certificate is given—

(a) may not reject the certificate except on prescribed grounds, and

(b) shall reject the certificate if any of the prescribed grounds exists.

(7) Unless, within the prescribed period, the local authority to whom a plans certificate is given give notice of rejection, specifying the ground or grounds in question, to—

(a) the approved inspector by whom the certificate was given, and

(b) the other person to whom the approved inspector gave the certificate,

the authority shall be conclusively presumed to have accepted the certificate.

(8) If it appears to a local authority by whom a plans certificate has been accepted that the work to which the certificate relates has not been commenced within the period of three years beginning on the date on which the certificate was accepted, the authority may rescind their acceptance of the certificate by notice, specifying the ground or grounds in question, given—

(a) to the approved inspector by whom the certificate was given, and

(b) to the person shown in the initial notice concerned as the person intending to carry out the work.

51 Final certificates

(1) Where an approved inspector is satisfied that any work specified in an initial notice given by him has been completed, he shall give—

(a) to the local authority by whom the initial notice was accepted, and

(b) to the person by whom the work was carried out,

such certificate with respect to the completion of the work and the discharge of his functions as may be prescribed (called a " final certificate ").

(2) Section 50(5) to (7) above has effect in relation to a final certificate as if any reference in those subsections to a plans certificate were a reference to a final certificate.

(3) Where a final certificate—

(a) has been given with respect to any of the work specified in an initial notice, and

(b) has been accepted by the local authority concerned,

the initial notice ceases to apply to that work, but section 48(1) above continues to apply, by virtue of this subsection, in relation to that work as if the initial notice continued in force in relation to it.

52 Cancellation of initial notice

(1) If, at a time when an initial notice is in force—

(a) the approved inspector becomes or expects to become unable to carry out (or to continue to carry out) his functions with respect to any of the work specified in the initial notice,

(b) the approved inspector is of the opinion that any of the work is being so carried out that he is unable adequately to carry out his functions with respect to it, or

(c) the approved inspector is of the opinion that there is a contravention of any provision of building regulations with respect to any of that work and the circumstances are as mentioned in subsection (2) below,

the approved inspector shall cancel the initial notice by notice in the prescribed form given to the local authority concerned and to the person carrying out or intending to carry out the work.

(2) The circumstances referred to in subsection (1)(c) above are—

(a) that the approved inspector has, in accordance with building regulations, given notice of the contravention to the person carrying out the work, and

(b) that, within the prescribed period, that person has neither pulled down nor removed the work nor effected such alterations in it as may be necessary to make it comply with building regulations.

(3) If, at a time when an initial notice is in force, it appears to the person carrying out or intending to carry out the work specified in the notice that the approved inspector is no longer willing or able to carry out his functions with respect to any of that work, he shall cancel the initial notice by notice in the prescribed form given to the local authority concerned and, if it is practicable to do so, to the approved inspector.

(4) If a person fails without reasonable excuse to give to a local authority a notice that he is required to give by subsection (3) above, he is liable on summary conviction to a fine not exceeding level 5 on the standard scale.

(5) If, at a time when an initial notice is in force, it appears to the local authority by whom the initial notice was accepted that the work to which the initial notice relates has not been commenced within the period of three years beginning on the date on which the initial notice was accepted, the authority may cancel the initial notice by notice in the prescribed form given—

(a) to the approved inspector by whom the initial notice was given, and

(b) to the person shown in the initial notice as the person intending to carry out the work.

(6) A notice under subsection (1), (3) or (5) above has the effect of cancelling the initial notice to which it relates with effect from the day on which the notice is given.

53 Effect of initial notice ceasing to be in force

(1) This section applies where an initial notice ceases to be in force by virtue of section 47(4)(b)(i) or (ii) above.

(2) Building regulations may provide that, if—

(a) a plans certificate was given before the day on which the initial notice ceased to be in force,

(b) that certificate was accepted by the local authority (before, on or after that day), and

(c) before that day, that acceptance was not rescinded by a notice under section 50(8) above,

then, with respect to the work specified in the certificate, such of the functions of a local authority referred to in section 48(1) above as may be prescribed for the purposes of this subsection either are not exercisable or are exercisable only in prescribed circumstances.

(3) If, before the day on which the initial notice ceased to be in force, a final certificate—

(a) was given in respect of part of the work specified in the initial notice, and

(b) was accepted by the local authority (before, on or after that day),

the fact that the initial notice has ceased to be in force does not affect the continuing operation of section 51(3) above in relation to that part of the work.

(4) Notwithstanding anything in subsections (2) and (3) above, for the purpose of enabling the local authority to perform the functions referred to in section 48(1) above in relation to any part of the work not specified in a plans certificate or final certificate, as the case may be, building regulations may require the local authority to be provided with plans that relate not only to that part but also to the part to which the certificate in question relates.

(5) In any case where this section applies, the reference in subsection (4) of section 36 above to the date of the completion of the work in question has effect, in relation to a notice under subsection (1) of that section, as if it were a reference to the date on which the initial notice ceased to be in force.

(6) Subject to any provision of building regulations made by virtue of subsection (2) above, if, before the initial notice ceased to be in force, an offence under section 35 above was committed with respect to any of the work specified in that notice, proceedings for that offence may be commenced by the local authority at any time within six months beginning with the day on which the function of the local authority referred to in section 48(1) above became exercisable with respect to the provision of building regulations to which the offence relates.

(7) The fact that an initial notice has ceased to be in force does not affect the right to give a new initial notice relating to any of the work that was specified in the original notice and in respect of which no final certificate has been given and accepted ; but where—

(a) a plans certificate has been given in respect of any of that work,

(b) the conditions in paragraphs (a) to (c) of subsection (2) above are fulfilled with respect to that certificate, and

(c) such a new initial notice is given and accepted,

section 50(1) above does not apply in relation to so much of the work to which the new initial notice relates as is work specified in the plans certificate.

Supervision of their own work by public bodies

54 Giving, acceptance and effect of public body's notice

(1) This section applies where a body (corporate or unincorporated) that acts under an enactment for public purposes and not for its own profit and is, or is of a description that is, approved by the Secretary of State in accordance with building regulations (in this Part of this Act referred to as a " public body ")—

(a) intends to carry out in relation to a building belonging to it work to which the substantive requirements of building regulations apply,

(b) considers that the work can be adequately supervised by its own servants or agents, and

(c) gives to the local authority in whose district the work is to be carried out notice in the prescribed form (called a "public body's notice") together with such plans of the work as may be prescribed.

(2) A public body's notice is of no effect unless it is accepted by the local authority to whom it is given; and that local authority—

(a) may not reject the notice except on prescribed grounds, and

(b) shall reject the notice if any of the prescribed grounds exists,

and, in a case where the work to which the public body's notice relates is work of such a description that, if plans of it had been deposited with the local authority, the authority could, under an enactment, have imposed requirements as a condition of passing the plans, the local authority may impose the like requirements as a condition of accepting the public body's notice.

(3) Unless, within the prescribed period, the local authority to whom a public body's notice is given give notice of rejection, specifying the ground or grounds in question, the authority is conclusively presumed to have accepted the public body's notice and to have done so without imposing any such requirements as are referred to in subsection (2) above.

(4) Section 48 above has effect for the purposes of this section—

(a) with the substitution of a reference to a public body's notice for any reference to an initial notice, and

(b) with the substitution, in subsection (2)(a), of a reference to subsection (1)(c) of this section for the reference to section 47(1)(b).

(5) The form prescribed for a public body's notice may be such as to require the public body by whom it is to be given—

(a) to furnish information relevant for the purposes of this Act, Part II or IV of the Public Health Act 1936 or any provision of building regulations, and

(b) to enter into undertakings with respect to consultation and other matters.

(6) Where a public body's notice is given and accepted by the local authority to whom it is given, the provisions of Schedule 4 to this Act have effect, being provisions that correspond, as nearly as may be, to those made by the preceding provisions of this Part of this Act for the case where an initial notice is given and accepted.

Supplementary

55 Appeals

(1) A person aggrieved by the local authority's rejection of—

(a) an initial notice or a public body's notice, or

(b) a plans certificate, a final certificate, a public body's plans certificate or a public body's final certificate,

may appeal to a magistrates' court acting for the petty sessions area in which is situated land on which there will be, or there has been, carried out any work to which the notice or certificate relates.

(2) On an appeal under subsection (1) above, the court shall—

(a) if it determines that the notice or certificate was properly rejected, confirm the rejection, and

(b) in any other case, give a direction to the local authority to accept the notice or certificate.

(3) Where a person is aggrieved by a determination, confirmation, direction or other decision of a magistrates' court under this section, he may appeal to the Crown Court.

56 Recording and furnishing of information

(1) Every local authority shall keep, in such manner as may be prescribed, a register containing such information as may be prescribed with respect to initial notices, public body's notices and certificates given to them, including information as to whether such notices or certificates have been accepted or rejected.

(2) The information that may be prescribed under subsection (1) above with respect to an initial notice includes information about the insurance cover provided with respect to the work to which the initial notice relates.

(3) The reference in subsection (1) above to certificates is a reference to plans certificates, final certificates, public body's plans certificates, public body's final certificates and certificates given under section 16(9) above.

(4) Every register kept under this section shall be available for inspection by the public at all reasonable hours.

(5) Where an initial notice or a public body's notice has continued in force for any period, the local authority by whom it was accepted may require the approved inspector or public body by whom it was given to furnish them with any information that—

(a) they would have obtained themselves if during that period their function of enforcing building regulations had continued to be exercisable in relation to the work specified in the notice, and

(b) they require for the purpose of performing their duty under section 230 of the Local Government Act 1972 (reports and returns), and that section shall have effect as if during that period that function had continued to be so exercisable.

57 Offences

(1) If a person—

(a) gives a notice or certificate that—

(i) purports to comply with the requirements of this Part of this Act or, as the case may be, of section 16(9) above, and

(ii) contains a statement that he knows to be false or misleading in a material particular, or

(b) recklessly gives a notice or certificate that—

(i) purports to comply with those requirements, and

(ii) contains a statement that is false or misleading in a material particular,

he is guilty of an offence.

(2) A person guilty of an offence under subsection (1) above is liable—

(a) on summary conviction, to a fine not exceeding the statutory maximum or imprisonment for a term not exceeding six months or both, and

(b) on conviction on indictment, to a fine or imprisonment for a term not exceeding two years or both.

(3) Where an approved inspector or person approved for the purposes of section 16(9) above is convicted of an offence under this section, the court by or before which he is convicted shall, within one month of the date of conviction, forward a certificate of the conviction to the person by whom the approval was given.

58 Construction of Part II

(1) In this Part of this Act—

" final certificate " has the meaning given by section 51(1) above;

" initial notice " has the meaning given by section 47(1) above;

" plans certificate " has the meaning given by section 50(1) above;

" public body " and " public body's notice " have the meanings given by section 54(1) above;

" public body's final certificate " has the meaning given by paragraph 3 of Schedule 4 to this Act;

" public body's plans certificate " has the meaning given by paragraph 2 of Schedule 4 to this Act.

(2) A reference in this Part of this Act to the carrying out of work includes a reference to the making of a material change of use, as defined by and for the purposes of building regulations.

(3) A reference in this Part of this Act to an initial notice given by an approved inspector is a reference to a notice given by him jointly with another person as mentioned in section 47(1)(a) above.

PART III

OTHER PROVISIONS ABOUT BUILDINGS

Drainage

59 Drainage of building

(1) If it appears to a local authority that in the case of a building—

(a) satisfactory provision has not been, and ought to be, made for drainage as defined in section 21(2) above,

(b) a cesspool, private sewer, drain, soil pipe, rain-water pipe, spout, sink or other necessary appliance provided for the building is insufficient or, in the case of a private sewer or drain communicating directly or indirectly with a public sewer, is so defective as to admit subsoil water,

(c) a cesspool or other such work or appliance as aforesaid provided for the building is in such a condition as to be prejudicial to health or a nuisance, or

(d) a cesspool, private sewer or drain formerly used for the drainage of the building, but no longer used for it, is prejudicial to health or a nuisance,

they shall by notice require the owner of the building to make satisfactory provision for the drainage of the building, or, as the case may be, require either the owner or the occupier of the building to do such work as may be necessary for renewing, repairing or cleansing the existing cesspool, sewer, drain, pipe, spout, sink or other appliance, or for filling up, removing or otherwise rendering innocuous the disused cesspool, sewer or drain.

(2) Sections 99 and 102 below apply in relation to a notice given under subsection (1) above.

(3) Subsections (4), (5) and (6) of section 21 above apply in relation to a drain that a local authority require to be constructed under this section as they apply in relation to such a proposed drain as is mentioned in that section.

(4) Subsection (1) above, so far as it empowers a local authority to take action in the cases mentioned in paragraphs (a) and (b) of the subsection, does not apply in relation to a building belonging to statutory undertakers, the British Airports Authority or the Civil Aviation Authority and held or used by them for the purposes of their undertaking, unless it is—

(a) a house, or in the case of the British Airports Authority a house or a hotel, or

(b) a building used as offices or showrooms, and not forming part of a railway station or in the case of the British Airports Authority or the Civil Aviation Authority not being on an aerodrome owned by the Authority in question.

60 Use and ventilation of soil pipes

(1) A pipe for conveying rain-water from a roof shall not be used for the purpose of conveying the soil or drainage from a sanitary convenience.

(2) The soil pipe from a water-closet shall be properly ventilated.

(3) A pipe for conveying surface water from premises shall not be permitted to act as a ventilating shaft to a drain or sewer conveying foul water.

(4) If it appears to the local authority or the water authority for the area that there is on any premises a contravention of any provision of this section, they may by notice require the owner or the occupier of those premises to execute such work as may be necessary to remedy the matter.

(5) Sections 99 and 102 below apply in relation to a notice given under subsection (4) above.

61 Repair etc. of drain

(1) No person shall—

(a) except in case of emergency, repair, reconstruct or alter the course of an underground drain that communicates with a sewer, or with a cesspool or other receptacle for drainage, or

(b) where in a case of emergency any such works have been executed without notice, cover over the drain or sewer,

without giving to the local authority at least 24 hours' notice of his intention to do so.

(2) While any such work as aforesaid is being executed, all persons concerned shall permit the proper officer, or any other authorised officer, of the local authority to have free access to the work.

(3) A person who fails to comply with this section is liable on summary conviction to a fine not exceeding level 3 on the standard scale.

(4) This section does not apply to—

(a) so much of a drain or sewer constructed by, or belonging to, a railway company as runs under, across or along their railway, or

(b) so much of a drain or sewer constructed by, or belonging to, dock undertakers as is situated in or on land of the undertakers that is held or used by them for the purposes of their undertaking.

62 Disconnection of drain

(1) Where a person—

(a) reconstructs in the same or a new position a drain that communicates with a sewer or another drain,

(b) executes any works to such a drain so as permanently to discontinue its use, or

(c) executes any works on premises served by such a drain so as permanently to discontinue its use,

he shall cause any drains or parts of drains thereby becoming disused or unnecessary to be disconnected and sealed at such points as the local authority may reasonably require.

(2) Any question as to the reasonableness of a requirement of a local authority under this section shall be determined by a magistrates' court, and the court may vary the requirement as it minks fit.

(3) No one shall be required under this section to carry out any work in land outside the premises served by the drain if he has no right to carry out that work, but, subject to section 101 below, the person undertaking the reconstruction of the drain or the

execution of the works may break open any street for the purpose of complying with a requirement under this section.

(4) Before a person complies with a requirement under this section, he shall give at least 48 hours' notice to the local authority, and a person who fails to comply with this subsection is liable on summary conviction to a fine not exceeding level 1 on the standard scale.

(5) A person who knowingly fails to comply with subsection (1) above is liable on summary conviction to a fine not exceeding level 1 on the standard scale and to a further fine not exceeding £1 for each day on which the default continues after he is convicted.

(6) This section does not apply in relation to anything done in the course of the demolition of a building, or of part of a building, being a demolition as respects which the local authority have power under section 81 below to serve a notice on the person undertaking the demolition.

63 Improper construction or repair of water-closet or drain

(1) If a water-closet, drain or soil pipe is so constructed or repaired as to be prejudicial to health or a nuisance, the person who undertook or executed the construction or repair is fable on summary conviction to a fine not exceeding level 1 on the standard scale, unless he shows that the prejudice to health or nuisance could not have been avoided by the exercise of reasonable care.

(2) A person charged with an offence under this section (hereafter in this section referred to as " the original defendant") is entitled, upon information duly laid by him and on giving to the prosecutor not less than three clear days' notice of his intention, to have any other person, being his agent or servant, to whose act or default he alleges that the offence was due brought before the court at the time appointed for the hearing of the charge ; and—

- (a) if after the commission of the offence has been proved the original defendant proves that the offence was due to the act or default of that other person, that other person may be convicted of the offence, and
- (b) if the original defendant further proves that he used all due diligence to secure that the water-closet, drain or soil pipe in question was so constructed or repaired as not to be prejudicial to health or a nuisance, he shall be acquitted of the offence.

(3) Where the original defendant seeks to avail himself of subsection (2) above—

- (a) the prosecutor as well as the person whom the original defendant charges with the offence has the right to cross-examine the original defendant, if he gives evidence, and any witness called by him in support of his pleas, and to call rebutting evidence, and
- (b) the court may make such order as it thinks fit for the payment of costs by any party to the proceedings to any other party to them.

(4) In this section in its application to Greater London, a reference to a water-closet includes a reference to a urinal.

Provision of sanitary conveniences

64 Provision of closets in building

(1) If it appears to a local authority—

(a) that a building is without sufficient closet accommodation,

(b) that a part of a building, being a part that is occupied as a separate dwelling, is without sufficient closet accommodation, or

(c) that any closets provided for or in connection with a building are in such a state as to be prejudicial to health or a nuisance and cannot without reconstruction be put into a satisfactory condition,

the authority shall, by notice to the owner of the building, require him to provide the building with such closets or additional closets, or such substituted closets, being in each case either water-closets or earth-closets, as may be necessary.

(2) Unless a sufficient water supply and sewer are available, the authority shall not require the provision of a water-closet except in substitution for an existing water-closet.

(3) Sections 99 and 102 below apply in relation to a notice given under subsection (1) above.

(4) Among the grounds on which an appeal may be brought under section 102 below against such a notice is that—

(a) the need for the works to be executed under the notice would not, in whole or in part, arise but for the occupation of part of the building as a separate dwelling, and the occupation of that part as a separate dwelling is a matter in respect of which the appellant has a cause of action, and

(b) the person against whom the appellant has a cause of action ought to contribute towards the expenses of executing the works.

(5) Where the grounds on which an appeal under section 102 below is brought include the ground specified in subsection (4) above—

(a) the appellant shall serve a copy of his notice of appeal on the person or persons referred to in that ground of appeal, and

(b) on the hearing of the appeal the court may make such order as it thinks fit with respect to—

(i) the contribution to be made by any such person towards the cost of the works, or

(ii) the proportion in which any expenses that may be recoverable by the local authority are to be borne by the appellant and any such other person.

(6) This section does not apply to—

(a) a factory,

(b) a building that is used as a workplace, or

(c) premises to which the Offices, Shops and Railway Premises Act 1963 applies.

65 Provision of sanitary conveniences in workplace

(1) A building that is used as a workplace shall be provided with—

(a) sufficient and satisfactory accommodation in the way of sanitary conveniences, regard being had to the number of persons employed in, or in attendance at, the building, and

(b) where persons of both sexes are employed or in attendance, sufficient and satisfactory separate accommodation for persons of each sex, unless the local authority are satisfied that in the circumstances of the particular case the provision of such separate accommodation is unnecessary.

(2) If it appears to the local authority that subsection (1) above is not complied with in the case of any building, they shall by notice require the owner or the occupier of the building to make such alterations in the existing conveniences, and to provide such additional conveniences, as may be necessary.

(3) Sections 99 and 102 below apply in relation to a notice given under subsection (2) above.

(4) This section does not apply to premises to which the Offices, Shops and Railway Premises Act 1963 applies.

66 Replacement of earth-closets etc.

(1) If a building has a sufficient water supply and sewer available, the local authority may, subject to this section, by notice to the owner of the building require that any closets, other than water-closets, provided for, or in connection with, the building shall be replaced by water-closets, notwithstanding that the closets are not insufficient in number and are not prejudicial to health or a nuisance.

(2) A notice under subsection (1) above shall—

(a) require the owner to execute the necessary works, or

(b) require that the authority themselves shall be allowed to execute them,

and shall state the effect of subsection (3) below.

(3) Where the local authority give a notice under subsection (1) above—

(a) if it requires the owner to execute the works, the owner is entitled to recover from them one-half of the expenses reasonably incurred by him in the execution of the works, and

(b) if it requires that they shall be allowed to execute the works, they are entitled to recover from the owner one-half of the expenses reasonably incurred by them in the execution of the works.

(4) Where the owner of a building proposes to provide it with a water-closet in substitution for a closet of any other type, the local authority may, if they think fit, agree to pay him a part, not exceeding one-half, of the expenses reasonably incurred in effecting the replacement, notwithstanding that a notice has not been given by them under subsection (1) above.

(5) Sections 99 and 102 below apply in relation to a notice given under subsection (1) above, subject to the following modifications—

(a) no appeal lies on the ground that the works are unnecessary, and

(b) any reference in the said section 99 to the expenses reasonably incurred in executing works is a reference to one-half of those expenses.

67 Loan of temporary sanitary conveniences

(1) A local authority may, at the request of the occupier of any premises connected with a cesspool, sewer or drain on which any work of maintenance, improvement or repair that necessitates the disconnection of the sanitary conveniences provided for or in connection with the premises is to be carried out—

(a) by a local authority, or

(b) by the owner or occupier of the premises in pursuance of section 59 above, supply on loan temporary sanitary conveniences in substitution for any sanitary conveniences so disconnected.

(2) Subject to the following provisions of this section, the local authority may make reasonable charges for supplying, removing and cleansing any temporary sanitary conveniences lent under this section for more than seven days.

(3) No charge may be made under subsection (2) above—

(a) for the use of the temporary sanitary conveniences for the first seven days, or

(b) in a case where the work is made necessary by a defect in a public sewer vested in and maintainable by the local authority (not being a length of sewer to which subsection (4) below applies).

(4) No charge may be made under subsection (2) above where the work is made necessary—

(a) by a defect in a length of a public sewer of a kind described in section 24(4) of the Public Health Act 1936 (which relates to sewers for the maintenance of which a local authority may make the owners of the premises served by the sewers pay), or

(b) by a defect in a cesspool, private sewer or drain in respect of which the local authority have served a notice under section 59 above,

but, if the temporary sanitary conveniences are provided for a period of more than seven days, the reasonable expenses of supplying, removing and cleansing them are recoverable from the owner of the premises (but not any charge for the use of them for the first seven days).

(5) In proceedings to recover expenses under subsection (4) above, the court may—

(a) inquire whether the expenses ought to be borne wholly or in part by some person other than the defendant in the proceedings, and

(b) make such order concerning the expenses or their apportionment as appears to the court to be just,

but the court shall not order the expenses or any part of them to be borne by any person other than the defendant in the proceedings unless the court is satisfied that that other person has had notice of the proceedings and an opportunity of being heard.

68 Erection of public conveniences

(1) No person shall erect a public sanitary convenience in, or so as to be accessible from, a street without the consent of the local authority, who may give their consent upon such terms as to the use of the convenience or its removal at any time, if required by them, as they think fit.

(2) A person who contravenes subsection (1) above is liable on summary conviction to a fine not exceeding level 1 on the standard scale, without prejudice to the right of the authority under subsection (4) below to require the convenience to be removed.

(3) A person aggrieved by the refusal of a local authority to give a consent under subsection (1) above, or by any terms imposed by them, may appeal to a magistrates' court.

(4) The local authority may by notice require—

(a) the owner of a sanitary convenience—

(i) that has been erected in contravention of subsection (1) above, or

(ii) that the authority are, by virtue of the terms of a consent given under that subsection, entitled to require to be removed, to remove it, or

(b) the owner of a sanitary convenience that opens on a street, and is so placed or constructed as to be a nuisance or offensive to public decency, to remove it or permanently close it.

(5) Sections 99 and 102 below apply in relation to a notice given under subsection (4) above.

(6) In this section, a reference to a local authority, in relation to a street that is a highway for which the local authority are not the highway authority, is a reference to the highway authority.

(7) Subsection (1) above does not apply to a sanitary convenience erected—

(a) by a railway company within their railway station or its yard or approaches, or

(b) by dock undertakers in or on land that belongs to them and is held or used by them for the purposes of their undertaking.

(8) This section does not affect the powers of—

(a) a county council or the Greater London Council under section 87 of the Public Health Act 1936,

(b) the Secretary of State under section 112 of the Highways Act 1980, or

(c) a county council under section 114(1) of the Highways Act 1980.

Buildings

69 Provision of water supply in occupied house

(1) Where a local authority are satisfied that an occupied house has not a supply of wholesome water in pipes in the house sufficient for the domestic purposes of the occupants, the local authority may—

(a) if they are satisfied that in all the circumstances it is reasonable to require the owner of the house to connect it to a supply of water in pipes provided by statutory water undertakers, give notice to the owner requiring him to connect the house as aforesaid, or

(b) if they are not satisfied that it is reasonable in all the circumstances to require the owner to connect the house as aforesaid, but are satisfied that it is reasonable to require him otherwise to take water into the house by means of a pipe, give notice to the owner requiring him so to take water into the house,

within a time specified in the notice.

(2) Where a local authority are satisfied that—

(a) an occupied house has not within a reasonable distance of it a supply of wholesome water sufficient for the domestic purposes of the occupants, and

(b) in all the circumstances it is not reasonable to require the owner to connect the house, or to take water into the house, as aforesaid,

the authority may give notice to the owner requiring him to provide a sufficient supply of wholesome water within a reasonable distance of the house within a time specified in the notice.

(3) Where the local authority are so satisfied as aforesaid with respect to each of two or more houses, and are further satisfied that the needs of those houses can most convenientlly be met by means of a joint supply, they may give notice accordingly under either subsection (1) or subsection (2) above to the owners of all those houses.

(4) If a person to whom a notice has been given under this section objects to the requirement of the local authority, he may, within 28 days after service on him of the notice, appeal to a magistrates' court, and, upon any such appeal, the court may either disallow the requirement of the local authority or allow it with or without modifications.

(5) If a requirement contained in a notice given under this section, including a requirement modified by the court under subsection (4) above, is not complied with—

(a) within the time specified in the notice, or

(b) if the court extends that time, within the time as so extended,

the local authority may themselves provide, or secure the provision of, a supply of water to the house or houses in question and may recover any expenses reasonably incurred by them in so doing from—

(i) the owner of the house, or

(ii) where two or more houses are concerned, the owners of those houses in such proportions as may be determined by the authority or, in case of dispute, by a magistrates' court,

but an owner shall not be required to pay more than £300 in respect of any one house.

(6) The Secretary of State may by order increase the amount specified in subsection (5) above, and where such an order is made—

(a) the statutory instrument containing it is subject to annulment in pursuance of a resolution of either House of Parliament, and

(b) the order does not apply to a notice given under this section before the commencement of the order.

(7) Where—

(a) any houses with respect to which the local authority are, by reason of notices not having been complied with, in a position to take action under subsection (5) above are situated within the limits of supply of statutory water undertakers, and

(b) the aggregate amount of the water rates that would be payable annually by owners or occupiers of those houses at the rates charged by the undertakers is such that a requisition could be made by those owners or occupiers under section 29 of Schedule 3 to the Water Act 1945 or under that section as modified by any enactment regulating the undertaking,

the local authority may themselves make such a requisition, and the undertakers shall comply with it as if it had been made by the owners or occupiers of the houses, and those owners or occupiers are deemed to have made the requisition and to have entered into an agreement with the undertakers to take a supply of water for the minimum period mentioned in the said section, or in the said section as so modified.

(8) Where under this section a supply of water is furnished to a house by statutory water undertakers., water rates may be made on the premises and recovered as if the owner or occupier of the house had demanded and agreed to pay water rates for a supply.

(9) Where under this section two or more houses in the occupation of different persons are supplied with water by a common pipe belonging to the owners or occupiers of those houses or parts of houses, or to some of them, the local authority may—

- (a) when necessary, repair or renew the pipe, and
- (b) recover any expenses reasonably incurred, by them in doing so from the owners or occupiers of the houses in such proportions as may be determined by the authority or, in case of dispute, by a magistrates' court.

70 Provision of food storage accommodation in house

(1) If it appears to a local authority that a house, or part of a building that is occupied as a separate dwelling, is without sufficient and suitable accommodation for the storage of food, the local authority may by notice require the owner of the house or building to provide the house or building with sufficient and suitable accommodation for that purpose.

(2) Sections 99 and 102 below apply in relation to a notice given under subsection (1) above.

(3) Among the grounds on which an appeal may be brought under section 102 below against such a notice are—

- (a) that it is not reasonably practicable to comply with the notice;
- (b) that—
  - (i) the need for the works to be executed under the notice would not, in whole or in part, arise but for the occupation of part of the building as a separate dwelling, and that the occupation of that part as a separate dwelling is a matter in respect of which the appellant has a cause of action, and
  - (ii) the person against whom the appellant has a cause of action ought to contribute towards the expenses of executing the works.

(4) Where the grounds on which an appeal under section 102 below is brought include the ground specified in subsection (3)(b) above—

- (a) the appellant shall serve a copy of his notice of appeal on the person or persons referred to in that ground of appeal, and
- (b) on the hearing of the appeal the court may make such order as it thinks fit with respect to—
  - (i) the contribution to be made by any such person towards the cost of the works, or
  - (ii) the proportion in which any expenses that may be recoverable by the local authority are to be borne by the appellant and any such other person.

71 Entrances, exits etc. to be required in certain cases

(1) If it appears to a local authority that a building to which this section applies is not provided with such means of ingress and egress and passages or gangways as the

authority, after consultation with the fire authority, deem satisfactory, regard being had to—

(a) the purposes for which the building is used, and

(b) the number of persons likely to resort to it at any one time,

the authority shall by notice require the owner of the building to execute such work and make such provision in regard to the matters aforesaid as may be necessary.

(2) Sections 99 and 102 below apply in, relation to a notice given under subsection (1) above.

(3) If the authority are satisfied that the safety of the public requires that immediate action should be taken in the case of any building as respects which they have given a notice under subsection (1) above, they may apply to a magistrates' court, and the court may make such temporary order as it thinks fit for the closing of the building to, or for restricting its use by, the public

(4) The person having the control of any building to which this section applies shall take steps to secure that the means of ingress and egress and the passages and gangways, while persons are assembled in the building, are kept free and unobstructed, except in so far as the local authority may, after consultation with the fire authority, otherwise approve, and if he fails to do so he is liable on summary conviction to a fine not exceeding level 4 on the standard scale.

(5) This section applies to the buildings to which section 24 above applies.

(6) This section has effect subject to section 30(3) of the Fire Precautions Act 1971.

72 Means of escape from fire

(1) If it appears to a local authority, after consultation with the fire authority, that—

(a) a building to which this section applies is not provided, or

(b) a proposed building that will be a building to which this section applies will not be provided,

with such means of escape in case of fire as the local authority, after such consultation, deem necessary from each storey whose floor is more than twenty feet above the surface of the street or ground on any side of the building, the authority shall by notice require the owner of the building, or, as the case may be, the person proposing to erect the building, to execute such work or make such other provision in regard to the matters aforesaid as may be necessary.

(2) Sections 99 and 102 below apply in relation to a notice given under subsection (1) above in so far as it requires a person to execute works.

(3) In so far as such a notice requires a person to make provision otherwise than by the execution of works, he is, if he fails to comply with the notice, liable on summary conviction to a fine not exceeding level 4 on the standard scale and to a further fine not exceeding £2 for each day on which the offence continues after he is convicted.

(4) In proceedings under subsection (3) above, it is open to the defendant to question the reasonableness of the authority's requirements.

(5) Where building regulations imposing requirements as to the provision of means of escape in case of fire are applicable to a proposed building or proposed extension of a

building, or would be so applicable but for a direction under section 8 above dispensing with such requirements—

(a) this section, and

(b) any provision of a local Act that has effect in place of this section,

does not apply in relation to the proposed building or extension.

(6) This section applies to a building that exceeds two storeys in height and in which the floor of any upper storey is more than twenty feet above the surface of the street or ground on any side of the building and that—

(a) is let in flats or tenement dwellings,

(b) is used as an inn, hotel, boarding-house, hospital, nursing home, boarding-school, children's home or similar institution, or

(c) is used as a restaurant, shop, store or warehouse and has on an upper floor sleeping accommodation for persons employed on the premises.

(7) This section has effect subject to section 30(3) of the Fire Precautions Act 1971.

73 Raising of chimney

(1) Where, after the 3rd October 1961 (which was the date of commencement of the relevant provisions of the Public Health Act 1961)—

(a) a person erects or raises a building (in this section referred to as " the taller building ") to a greater height than an adjoining building, and

(b) any chimneys or flues of an adjoining building are in a party wall between the two buildings or are six feet or less from the nearest part of the taller building,

the local authority may by notice—

(i) require that person, within such time as may be specified in the notice, to build up those chimneys and flues, if it is reasonably practicable so to do, so that their top will be of the same height as the top of the chimneys of the taller building or the top of the taller building, whichever is the higher, and

(ii) require the owner or occupier of the adjoining building to allow the first-mentioned person to enter on that building and carry out such work as may be necessary to comply with the notice served on him,

except that, if the said owner or occupier, within fourteen days from the date of service of the notice on him, serves on the first-mentioned person and on the local authority a notice (in this section referred to as a " counter-notice ") that he elects to carry out the work himself, the owner or occupier shall comply with the notice served under paragraph (i) above instead of the first-mentioned person and may recover the expenses reasonably incurred in so doing from that person.

(2) A person on whom a notice is served under paragraph (i) or paragraph (ii) of subsection (1) above may appeal to a magistrates' court.

(3) If—

(a) a person on whom a notice is served under paragraph (i) of subsection (1) above fails to comply with the notice, except in a case where the owner or occupier of an adjoining building has refused to allow entry on that building, or has refused to allow the carrying out of any such work as may be necessary to comply with the notice, or has served a counter-notice, or

(b) a person on whom a notice is served under paragraph (ii) of subsection (1) above fails to comply with the notice or, having served a counter-notice, fails to comply with the notice served under paragraph (i) of that subsection,

he is liable on summary conviction to a fine not exceeding level 1 on the standard scale, and the local authority may themselves carry out such work as may be necessary to comply with the notice served under the said paragraph (1), and recover the expenses reasonably incurred in doing so from the person on whom that notice was served.

74 Cellars and rooms below subsoil water level

(1) No person shall without the consent of the local authority construct a cellar or room in, or as part of, a house, shop, inn, hotel or office if the floor level of the cellar or room is lower man the ordinary level of the subsoil water on, under or adjacent to the site of the house, shop, inn, hotel or office.

(2) Subsection (1) above does not apply to—

(a) the construction of a cellar or room carried out in accordance with plans deposited on an application under the Licensing Act 1964 to licensing justices on which they made a provisional grant of—

(i) a justices' licence for the premises of which the cellar or room forms part, or

(ii) a removal of a justices' licence to those premises, or

(b) the construction of a cellar or room in connection with a shop, inn, hotel or office that forms part of a railway station.

(3) If a person constructs a cellar or room in contravention of subsection (1) above, or of any condition attached to a consent under this section—

(a) he is liable on summary conviction to a fine not exceeding level 1 on the standard scale, and

(b) the local authority may by notice require him either to alter the cellar or room so that its construction will no longer contravene the said subsection or condition or, if he so elects, to fill it in or otherwise make it unusable.

(4) Sections 99 and 102 below apply in relation to a notice given under subsection (3) above, subject to the following modifications—

(a) section 99(1) requires the notice to indicate the nature of the works of alteration and that of the works for making the cellar or room unusable, and

(b) section 99(2) authorises the local authority to execute, subject to that subsection, at their election either the works of alteration or the works for making the cellar or room unusable.

(5) If the owner for the time being of the house, shop, inn, hotel or office causes or permits a cellar or room forming part of it to be used in a manner that he knows to be in contravention of a condition attached to a consent under this section, he is liable on summary conviction to a fine not exceeding level 1 on the standard scale.

75 Consents under s. 74

(1) A consent under section 74 above may be given subject to such conditions as to the construction or use of the premises as may be specified in it, and conditions specified in such a consent are binding on successive owners of the house, shop, inn, hotel or office.

(2) If a local authority—

(a) refuse an application for such a consent, or

(b) attach any conditions to such a consent,

the person applying for the consent may appeal to a magistrates' court against the refusal or, as the case may be, against any of the conditions, and if a magistrates' court allows an appeal against a refusal to grant a consent it may direct the local authority to give their consent subject to such conditions, if any, as appear to the court to be appropriate.

(3) An application may be made at any time to the local authority for the variation or withdrawal of a condition attached to such a consent, and, if the local authority refuse the application, the applicant may appeal to a magistrates' court.

Defective premises, demolition etc.

76 Defective premises

(1) If it appears to a local authority that—

(a) any premises are in such a state (in this section referred to as a " defective state ") as to be prejudicial to health or a nuisance, and

(b) unreasonable delay in remedying the defective state would be occasioned by following the procedure prescribed by sections 93 to 96 of the Public Health Act 1936,

the local authority may serve on the person on whom it would have been appropriate to serve an abatement notice under the said section 93 (if the local authority had proceeded under that section) a notice stating that the local authority intend to remedy the defective state and specifying the defects that they intend to remedy.

(2) Subject to subsection (3) below, the local authority may, after the expiration of nine days after service of a notice under subsection (1) above, execute such works as may be necessary to remedy the defective state, and recover the expenses reasonably incurred in so doing from the person on whom the notice was served.

(3) If, within seven days after service of a notice under subsection (1) above, the person on whom the notice was served serves a counter-notice that he intends to remedy the defects specified in the first-mentioned notice, the local authority shall take no action in pursuance of the first-mentioned, notice unless the person who served the counter-notice—

(a) fails within what seems to the local authority a reason able time to begin to execute works to remedy the said defects, or

(b) having begun to execute such works fails to make such progress towards their completion as seems to the local authority reasonable.

(4) In proceedings to recover expenses under subsection (2) above, the court—

(a) shall inquire whether the local authority were justified in concluding that the premises were in a defective state, or that unreasonable delay in remedying the defective state would have been occasioned by following the procedure prescribed by sections 93 to 96 of the Public Health Act 1936, and

(b) if the defendant proves that he served a counter-notice under subsection (3) above, shall inquire whether the defendant failed to begin the works to remedy the defects within a reasonable time, or failed to make reasonable progress towards their completion,

and if the court determines that—

(i) the local authority were not justified in either of the conclusions mentioned in paragraph (a) of this subsection, or

(ii) there was no failure under paragraph (b) of this subsection,

the local authority shall not recover the expenses or any part of them.

(5) Subject to subsection (4) above, in proceedings to recover expenses under subsection (2) above, the court may—

(a) inquire whether the said expenses ought to be borne wholly or in part by some person other than the defendant in the proceedings, and

(b) make such order concerning the expenses or their apportionment as appears to the court to be just,

but the court shall not order the expenses or any part of them to be borne by a person other than the defendant in the proceedings unless the court is satisfied that that other person has had due notice of the proceedings and an opportunity of being heard.

(6) A local authority shall not serve a notice under subsection (1) above, or proceed with the execution of works in accordance with a notice so served, if the execution of the works would, to their knowledge, be in contravention of a building preservation order under section 29 of the Town and Country Planning Act 1947.

(7) The power conferred on a local authority by subsection (1) above may be exercised notwithstanding that the local authority might instead have proceeded under section 9 of the Housing Act 1957.

77 Dangerous building

(1) If it appears to a local authority that a building or structure, or part of a building or structure, is in such a condition, or is used to carry such loads, as to be dangerous, the authority may apply to a magistrates' court, and the court may—

(a) where danger arises from the condition of the building or structure, make an order requiring the owner thereof—

(i) to execute such work as may be necessary to obviate die danger or,

(ii) if he so elects, to demolish the building or structure, or any dangerous part of it, and remove any rubbish resulting from the demolition, or

(b) where danger arises from overloading of the building or structure, make an order restricting its use until a magistrates' court, being satisfied that any necessary works have been executed, withdraws or modifies the restriction.

(2) If the person on whom an order is made under subsection (1)(a) above fails to comply with the order within the time specified, the local authority may—

(a) execute the order in such manner as they think fit, and

(b) recover the expenses reasonably incurred by them in doing so from the person in default,

and, without prejudice to the right of the authority to exercise those powers, the person is liable on summary conviction to a fine not exceeding level 1 on the standard scale.

78 Dangerous building-emergency measures

(1) If it appears to a local authority that—

(a) a building or structure, or part of a building or structure, is in such a state, or is used to carry such loads, as to be dangerous, and

(b) immediate action should be taken to remove the danger,

they may take such steps as may be necessary for that purpose.

(2) Before exercising their powers under this section, the local authority shall, if it is reasonably practicable to do so, give notice of their intention to the owner and occupier of the building, or of the premises on which the structure is situated.

(3) Subject to this section, the local authority may recover from the owner the expenses reasonably incurred by them under this section.

(4) So far as expenses incurred by the local authority under this section consist of expenses of fencing off the building or structure, or arranging for it to be watched, the expenses shall not be recoverable in respect of any period—

(a) after the danger has been removed by other steps under this section, or

(b) after an order made under section 77(1) above for the purpose of its removal has been complied with or has been executed as mentioned in subsection (2) of that section.

(5) In proceedings to recover expenses under this section, the court shall inquire whether the local authority might reasonably have proceeded instead under section 77(1) above, and, if the court determines that the local authority might reasonably have proceeded instead under that subsection, the local authority shall not recover the expenses or any part of them.

(6) Subject to subsection (5) above, in proceedings to recover expenses under this section, the court may—

(a) inquire whether the expenses ought to be borne wholly or in part by some person other than the defendant in the proceedings, and

(b) make such order concerning the expenses or their apportionment as appears to the court to be just,

but the court shall not order the expenses or any part of them to be borne by any person other than the defendant in the proceedings unless it is satisfied that that other person has had due notice of the proceedings and an opportunity of being heard.

(7) Where in consequence of the exercise of the powers conferred by this section the owner or occupier of any premises sustains damage, but section 106(1) below does not apply because the owner or occupier has been in default—

(a) the owner or occupier may apply to a magistrates' court to determine whether the local authority were justified in exercising their powers under this section so as to occasion the damage sustained, and

(b) if the court determines that the local authority were not so justified, the owner or occupier is entitled to compensation, and section 106(2) and (3) below applies in relation to any dispute as regards compensation arising under this subsection.

(8) The proper officer of a local authority may, as an officer of the local authority, exercise the powers conferred on the local authority by subsection (1) above.

(9) This section does not apply to premises forming part of a mine or quarry within the meaning of the Mines and Quarries Act 1954.

79 Ruinous and dilapidated buildings and neglected sites

(1) If it appears to a local authority that a building or structure is by reason of its ruinous or dilapidated condition seriously detrimental to the amenities of the neighbourhood, the local authority may by notice require the owner thereof—

(a) to execute such works of repair or restoration, or

(b) if he so elects, to take such steps for demolishing the building or structure, or any part thereof, and removing any rubbish or other material resulting from or exposed by the demolition,

as may be necessary in the interests of amenity.

(2) If it appears to a local authority that—

(a) rubbish or other material resulting from, or exposed by, the demolition or collapse of a building or structure is lying on the site or on any adjoining land, and

(b) by reason thereof the site or land is in such a condition as to be seriously detrimental to the amenities of the neighbourhood,

the local authority may by notice require the owner of the site or land to take such steps for removing the rubbish or material as may be necessary in the interests of amenity.

(3) Sections 99 and 102 below apply in relation to a notice given under subsection (1) or (2) above, subject to the following modifications—

(a) section 99(1) requires the notice to indicate the nature of the works of repair or restoration and that of the works of demolition and removal of rubbish or material, and

(b) section 99(2) authorises the local authority to execute, subject to that subsection, at their election either the works of repair or restoration or the works of demolition and removal of rubbish or material.

(4) This section does not apply to an advertisement as defined in section 290(1) of the Town and Country Planning Act 1971.

80 Notice to local authority of intended demolition

(1) This section applies to any demolition of the whole or part of a building except—

(a) a demolition in pursuance of a demolition order made under the Housing Act 1957, and

(b) a demolition—

(i) of an internal part of a building, where the building is occupied and it is intended that it should continue to be occupied,

(ii) of a building that has a cubic content. (as ascertained by external measurement) of not more than 1750 cubic feet, or, where a greenhouse, conservatory, shed or prefabricated garage forms part of a larger building, of that greenhouse, conservatory, shed or prefabricated garage, or

(iii) without prejudice to sub-paragraph (ii) above, of an agricultural building (as defined in section 26 of the General Rate Act 1967), unless it is contiguous to another building that is not itself an agricultural building or a building of a kind mentioned in that sub-paragraph.

(2) No person shall begin a demolition to which this section applies unless—

(a) he has given the local authority notice of his intention to do so, and

(b) either—

(i) the local authority have given a notice to him under section 81 below, or

(ii) the relevant period (as defined in that section) has expired.

(3) A notice under subsection (2) above shall specify the building to which it relates and the works of demolition intended to be carried out, and it is the duty of a person giving such a notice to a local authority to send or give a copy of it to—

(a) the occupier of any building adjacent to the building,

(b) the British Gas Corporation, and

(c) the Area Electricity Board in whose area the building is situated.

(4) A person who contravenes subsection (2) above is liable on summary conviction to a fine not exceeding level 4 on the standard scale.

81 Local authority's power to serve notice about demolition

(1) A local authority may give a notice under this section to—

(a) a person on whom a demolition order has been served under the Housing Act 1957,

(b) a person who appears to them not to be intending to comply with an order made under section 77 above or a notice given under section 79 above, and

(c) a person who appears to them to have begun or to be intending to begin a demolition to which section 80 above otherwise applies.

(2) Nothing contained in a notice under this section prejudices or affects the operation of any of the relevant statutory provisions, as defined in section 53(1) of the Health and Safety at Work etc. Act 1974; and accordingly, if a requirement of such a notice is inconsistent with a requirement imposed by or under the said Act of 1974, the latter requirement prevails.

(3) Where—

(a) a person has given a notice under section 80 above, or

(b) the local authority have served a demolition order on a person under the Housing Act 1957,

a notice under this section may only be given to the person in question within the relevant period.

(4) In this section and section 80 above, " the relevant period " means—

(a) in a case such as is mentioned in subsection (3)(a) above, six weeks from the giving of the notice under section 80 above, or such longer period as the person who gave that notice may in writing allow, and

(b) in a case such as is mentioned in subsection (3)(b) above, seven days after the local authority served a copy of the demolition order in accordance with the Housing Act 1957, or such longer period as the person on whom the copy was served may in writing allow.

(5) It is the duty of the local authority to send or give a copy of a notice under this section to the owner and occupier of any building adjacent to the building to which the notice relates.

(6) It is also the duty of the local authority to send or give a copy of a notice under this section—

(a) if it contains such a requirement as is specified in section 82(1)(h) below, to the statutory undertakers concerned, and

(b) if it contains such a requirement as is specified in section 82(1)(i) below—

(i) to the fire authority, if they are not themselves the fire authority, and

(ii) to the Health and Safety Executive, if the premises are special premises.

(7) In this section and section 82 below, " special premises " means premises for which a fire certificate is required by virtue of regulations under the Health and Safety at Work etc. Act 1974.

82 Notices under s. 81

(1) A notice under section 81(1) above may require the person to whom it is given—

(a) to shore up any building adjacent to the building to which die notice relates,

(b) to weatherproof any surfaces of an adjacent building that are exposed by the demolition,

(c) to repair and make good any damage to an adjacent building caused by the demolition or by the negligent act or omission of any person engaged in it,

(d) to remove material or rubbish resulting from the demolition and clearance of the site,

(e) to disconnect and seal, at such points as the local authority may reasonably require, any sewer or drain in or under the building,

(f) to remove any such sewer or drain, and seal any sewer or drain with which the sewer or drain to be removed is connected,

(g) to make good to the satisfaction of tile local authority the surface of the ground disturbed by anything done under paragraph (e) or (f) above,

(h) to make arrangements with the relevant statutory undertakers for the disconnection of the supply of gas, electricity and water to the building,

(i) to make such arrangements with regard to the burning of structures or materials on the site as may be reasonably required—

(i) if the building is or forms part of special premises, by the Health and Safety Executive and the fire authority, and

(ii) in any other case, by the fire authority, and

(j) to take such steps relating to die conditions subject to which the demolition is to be undertaken, and the condition in which the site is to be left on completion of the demolition, as the local authority may consider reasonably necessary for the protection of the public and the preservation of public amenity.

(2) No one shall be required under paragraph (c), (e) or (f) of subsection (1) above to carry out any work in land outside the premises on which the works of demolition are being carried out if he has no right to carry out that work, but, subject to section 101 below, the person undertaking the demolition, or the local authority acting in his default, may break open any street for the purpose of complying with any such requirement.

(3) Before a person complies with a requirement under paragraph (e), (f) or (g) of subsection (1) above, he shall give to the local authority—

(a) at least 48 hours' notice, in the case of a requirement under paragraph (e) or (f), or

(b) at least 24 hours' notice, in the case of a requirement under paragraph (g),

and a person who fails to comply with this subsection is liable on summary conviction to a fine not exceeding level 2 on the standard scale.

(4) This section does not authorise interference with apparatus or works of statutory undertakers authorised by an enactment to carry on an undertaking for the supply of electricity, gas or water.

(5) Without prejudice to the generality of subsection (4) above, this section does not exempt a person from—

(a) the obligation to obtain any consent required under section 67 of Schedule 3 to the Water Act 1945 (interference with valves and other apparatus) or section 68 of that Schedule (alterations to supply pipes and other apparatus),

(b) criminal liability under any enactment relating to the supply of gas or electricity, or

(c) the requirements of regulations under section 31 of the Gas Act 1972 (public safety).

(6) Section 99 below applies in relation to a notice given under section 81(1) above.

83 Appeal against notice under s. 81

(1) Section 102 below applies in relation to a notice given under section 81 above.

(2) Among the grounds on which an appeal may be brought under section 102 below against such a notice are—

(a) in the case of a notice requiring an adjacent building to be shored up, that the owner of the building is not entitled to the support of that building by the building that is being demolished, and ought to pay, or contribute towards, the expenses of shoring it up,

(b) in the case of a notice requiring any surfaces of an adjacent building to be weatherproofed, that the owner of the adjacent building ought to pay, or contribute towards, the expenses of weatherproofing those surfaces.

(3) Where the grounds on which an appeal under section 102 below is brought include a ground specified in subsection (2) above—

(a) the appellant shall serve a copy of his notice of appeal on the person or persons referred to in that ground of appeal, and

(b) on the hearing of the appeal the court may make such order as it thinks fit—

(i) in respect of the payment of, or contribution towards, the cost of the works by any such person, or

(ii) as to how any expenses that may be recoverable by the local authority are to be borne between the appellant and any such person.

Yards and passages

84 Paving and drainage of yards and passages

(1) If a court or yard appurtenant to, or a passage giving access to, buildings to which this section applies—

(a) is not so formed, flagged, asphalted or paved, or

(b) is not provided with such works on, above or below its surface,

as to allow of the satisfactory drainage of its surface or subsoil to a proper outfall, the local authority may by notice require any person who is the owner of any of the buildings to execute all such works as may be necessary to remedy the defect.

(2) Sections 99 and 102 below apply in relation to a notice given under subsection (1) above.

(3) The buildings to which this section applies are houses and industrial and commercial buildings.

(4) This section applies in relation to any court, yard or passage that is used in common by the occupiers of two or more houses, or a house and a commercial or industrial building, but is not a highway maintainable at the public expense.

85 Maintenance of entrances to courtyards

(1) Except with the consent of the local authority—

(a) an entrance to a court or yard on which two or more houses front or abut shall not be closed, narrowed, reduced in height or otherwise altered so as to impede the free circulation of air through the entrance, and

(b) no permanent structure shall be erected so as to impede the free circulation of air through such an entrance.

(2) A local authority in giving a consent under this section may impose such conditions as they think fit with respect to the provision of other openings or means of access, or other means for securing free circulation of air throughout the court or yard.

(3) A person aggrieved by the refusal of a local authority to give a consent under this section, or by a condition imposed by them, may appeal to a magistrates' court.

(4) A person who contravenes this section is liable on summary conviction to a fine not exceeding level 1 on the standard scale and to a further fine not exceeding £2 for each day on which the offence continues after he is convicted.

Appeal to Crown Court

86 Appeal to Crown Court

(1) Where a person—

(a) is aggrieved by an order, determination or other decision of a magistrates' court under this Part of this Act, or under Part IV of this Act as it applies in relation to this Part, and

(b) is not by any other enactment authorised to appeal to the Crown Court,

he may appeal to the Crown Court.

(2) Subsection (1) above does not confer a right of appeal in a case in which each of the parties concerned might under this Act have required that the dispute should be determined by arbitration instead of by a magistrates' court.

Application of provisions to Crown property

87 Application of provisions to Crown property

(1) This section applies to any house, building or other premises being property belonging to Her Majesty in right of the Crown or of the Duchy of Lancaster, or belonging to the Duchy of Cornwall, or belonging to a government department, or held in trust for Her Majesty for purposes of a government department

(2) In relation to any such property, the appropriate authority may agree with—

(a) the council of the county, or

(b) the local authority of the district,

in which the property is situated that any particular provisions of this Part of this Act, and of Part IV of this Act so far as it relates to this Part, shall apply to the property; and, while the agreement is in force, those provisions shall apply to that property accordingly, subject to the terms of the agreement.

(3) Any such agreement may contain such consequential and incidental provisions (including, with the approval of the Treasury, provisions of a financial character) as appear to the appropriate authority to be necessary or equitable.

(4) In this section, " the appropriate authority " means—

(a) in the case of property belonging to Her Majesty in right of the Crown, the Crown Estate Commissioners or other government department having the management of the property,

(b) in the case of property belonging to Her Majesty in right of the Duchy of Lancaster, the Chancellor of the Duchy,

(c) in the case of property belonging to the Duchy of Cornwall, such person as the Duke of Cornwall, or the possessor for the time being of the Duchy of Cornwall, appoints, and

(d) in the case of property belonging to a government department or held in trust for Her Majesty for purposes of a government department, that department,

and, if a question arises as to what authority is the appropriate authority in relation to any property, that question shall be referred to the Treasury, whose decision is final.

Inner London

88 Inner London

(1) In its application to inner London, this Part of this Act has effect subject to Part II of Schedule 3 to this Act.

(2) Part III of Schedule 3 to this Act has effect with respect to building and the drainage of buildings in the inner London boroughs.

(3) Part IV of Schedule 3 to this Act has effect with respect to the making of byelaws by the Greater London Council—

(a) for the inner London boroughs, with respect to certain matters, and
(b) for the inner London boroughs, the Inner Temple and the Middle Temple, with respect to certain other matters.

Miscellaneous

89 References in Acts to building byelaws

(1) Subject to subsection (2) below, for any reference to—
(a) building byelaws as defined in section 343 of the Public Health Act 1936, or
(b) byelaws made under Part II of that Act with respect to buildings, works and fittings,

that occurs in an Act, or in an instrument having effect under an Act, there is substituted a reference to building regulations.

(2) Subsection (1) above does not apply to the definition of "building byelaws" in section 189 of the Housing Act 1957, and a reference to building byelaws in section 12(4), 29(2) or 59(2) of that Act includes a reference to building regulations.

90 Facilities for inspecting local Acts

(1) In an area in which there is in force a local Act containing provisions that impose an obligation or restriction as to the construction, nature or situation of buildings, the local authority shall keep a copy of those provisions at their offices for inspection by the public at all reasonable times free of charge.

(2) Any question as to what provisions of a local Act are provisions of which a copy is to be so kept shall, on the application of the local authority, be determined by the Secretary of State.

PART IV

GENERAL

Duties of local authorities

91 Duties of local authorities

(1) It is the duty of local authorities to carry this Act into execution in their areas, subject to—
(a) the provisions of this Act relating to certain other authorities or persons,
(b) the provisions of Part I of the Public Health Act 1936 relating to united districts and joint boards,
(c) section 151 of the Local Government, Planning and Land Act 1980 (urban development areas), and
(d) section 1(3) of the Public Health (Control of Disease) Act 1984 (port health authorities).

(2) It is the function of local authorities to enforce building regulations in their areas, subject to sections 5(3), 48(1) and 53(2) above and (as to inner London) to Part V of Schedule 3 to this Act.

Documents

92 Form of documents

(1) All—

(a) notices, orders, consents, demands and other documents authorised or required by or under this Act to be given, made or issued by a local authority, and

(b) notices and applications authorised or required by or under this Act to be given or made to, or to any officer of, a local authority,

shall be in writing.

(2) The Secretary of State may, by regulations made by statutory instrument, prescribe the form of any notice, advertisement, certificate or other document to be used for any of the purposes of this Act, and if forms are so prescribed those forms or forms to the like effect may be used in all cases to which those forms are applicable.

93 Authentication of documents

(1) A notice, order, consent, demand or other document that a local authority are authorised or required by or under this Act to give, make or issue may be signed on behalf of the authority—

(a) by the proper officer of the authority or the district surveyor, as respects documents relating to matters within his province, or

(b) by an officer of the authority authorised by them in writing to sign documents of the particular kind or, as the case may be, the particular document.

(2) A document purporting to bear the signature of an officer—

(a) expressed to hold an office by virtue of which he is under this section empowered to sign such a document, or

(b) expressed to be authorised by the local authority to sign such a document or the particular document,

is deemed, for the purposes of this Act and of any building regulations and orders made under it, to have been duly given, made or issued by authority of the local authority, until the contrary is proved.

(3) In subsection (2) above, " signature " includes a facsimile of a signature by whatever process reproduced.

94 Service of documents

A notice, order, consent, demand or other document that is authorised or required by or under this Act to be given to or served on a person may, in any case for which no other provision is made by this Act, be given or served either—

(a) by delivering it to that person,

(b) in the case of an officer of a local authority, by leaving it, or sending it in a prepaid letter addressed to him, at his office,

(c) in the case of any other person, by leaving it, or sending it in a prepaid letter addressed to him, at his usual or last known residence,

(d) in the case of an incorporated company or body, by delivering it to their secretary or clerk at their registered or principal office, or by sending it in a prepaid letter addressed to him at that office,

(e) in the case of a document to be given to or served on a person as being the owner of any premises by virtue of the fact that he receives the rackrent thereof as agent for another, or would so receive it if the premises were let at a rackrent, by leaving it, or sending it in a prepaid letter addressed to him, at his place of business,

(f) in the case of a document to be given to or served on the owner or the occupier of any premises, if it is not practicable after reasonable inquiry to ascertain the name and address of the person to or on whom it should be given or served, or if the premises are unoccupied, by addressing it to the person concerned by the description of " owner " or " occupier " of the premises (naming them) to which it relates, and delivering it to some person on the premises, or, if there is no person on die premises to whom it can be delivered, by affixing it, or a copy of it, to some conspicuous part of the premises.

Entry on premises

95 Power to enter premises

(1) Subject to this section, an authorised officer of a local authority, on producing, if so required, some duly authenticated document showing his authority, has a right to enter any premises at all reasonable hours—

(a) for the purpose of ascertaining whether there is, or has been, on or in connection with the premises, a contravention of this Act, or of any building regulations, that it is the duty of the local authority to enforce,

(b) for the purpose of ascertaining whether or not circumstances exist that would authorise or require the local authority to take any action, or execute any work, under this Act or under building regulations,

(c) for the purpose of taking any action, or executing any work, authorised or required by this Act, or by building regulations, or by an order made under this Act, to be taken, or executed, by the local authority, or

(d) generally for the purpose of the performance by the local authority of their functions under this Act or under building regulations.

(2) Admission to premises, other than a factory or workplace, shall not be demanded as of right unless 24 hours' notice of the intended entry has been given to the occupier.

(3) If it is shown to the satisfaction of a justice of the peace on sworn information in writing that—

(a) admission to any premises has been refused, or refusal is apprehended, or the premises are unoccupied, or the occupier is temporarily absent, or the case is one of urgency, or an application for admission would defeat the object of the entry, and

(b) there is reasonable ground for entry into the premises for any of the purposes mentioned in subsection (1) above, the justice may by warrant under his hand authorise the local authority by any authorised officer to enter the premises, if need be by force.

(4) A warrant shall not be issued under subsection (3) above unless the justice is satisfied that—

(a) notice of the intention to apply for a warrant has been given to the occupier, or

(b) the premises are unoccupied, or the occupier is temporarily absent, or the case is one of urgency, or the giving of the notice would defeat the object of the entry.

96 Supplementary provisions as to entry

(1) An authorised officer entering premises by virtue of section 95 above, or of a warrant issued under it, may take with him such other persons as may be necessary, and on leaving unoccupied premises that he has entered by virtue of such a warrant he shall leave them as effectually secured against trespassers as he found them.

(2) A warrant issued under that section shall continue in force until the purpose for which the entry is necessary has been satisfied.

(3) A person who—

(a) is admitted into a factory or workplace in compliance with that section or a warrant issued under it, and

(b) discloses to another person information obtained by him in the factory or workplace with regard to a manufacturing process or trade secret,

is liable on summary conviction to a fine not exceeding level 3 on the standard scale or to imprisonment for a term not exceeding three months, unless the disclosure was made in the performance of his duty.

Execution of works

97 Power to execute work

A local authority may, by agreement with the owner or occupier of any premises, themselves execute at his expense—

(a) any work that they have under this Act required him to execute, or

(b) any work in connection with the construction, laying, alteration or repair of a sewer or drain that he is entitled to execute,

and for that purpose they have all the rights that he would have.

98 Power to require occupier to permit work

If, on a complaint made by the owner of premises, it appears to a magistrates' court that the occupier of those premises prevents the owner from executing any work that he is by or under this Act required to execute, the court may order the occupier to permit; the execution of the work.

99 Content and enforcement of notice requiring works

(1) A notice in relation to which it is declared by any provision of this Act that this section applies shall indicate the nature of the works to be executed and state the time within which they are to be executed.

(2) Subject to any right of appeal conferred by section 102 below, if the person required by such a notice to execute works fails to execute them within the time limited by the notice—

(a) the local authority may themselves execute the works and recover from that person the expenses reasonably incurred by them in doing so, and

(b) without prejudice to that power, he is liable on summary conviction to a fine not exceeding level 4 on the standard scale and to a further fine not exceeding £2 for each day on which the default continues after he is convicted.

(3) This section has effect subject to any modification specified in the provision under which the notice is given.

100 Sale of materials

(1) A local authority may sell any materials that—

(a) have been removed by them from any premises, including a street, when executing works under this Act or otherwise carrying this Act into effect, and

(b) are not before the expiration of three days from the date of their removal claimed by the owner and taken away by him.

(2) Where a local authority sell materials under this section, they shall pay the proceeds to the person to whom the materials belonged, after deducting the amount of any expenses recoverable by them from him.

(3) This section does not apply to refuse removed by a local authority.

101 Breaking open of streets

(1) For the purposes of any section of this Act that confers powers on local authorities to construct, lay or maintain sewers, drains or pipes, Part VI of the Third Schedule to the Water Act 1945 is incorporated with this Act, with such adaptations as may be necessary to make that Part applicable to the construction and maintenance of sewers and drains as well as to the laying and maintenance of water mains and pipes.

(2) The Part so incorporated with adaptations as aforesaid applies in relation to any person not being a local authority who is empowered by this Act to construct, lay or maintain a sewer or drain as if, so far as his powers extend, he were the undertakers.

Appeal against notice requiring works

102 Appeal against notice requiring works

(1) Where a person is given a notice in relation to which it is declared by any provision of this Act that this section applies, he may appeal to a magistrates' court on any of the following grounds that are appropriate in the circumstances of the particular case—

(a) that the notice or requirement is not justified by the terms of the provision under which it purports to have been given,

(b) that there has been some informality, defect or error in, or in connection with, the notice,

(c) that the authority have refused unreasonably to approve the execution of alternative works, or that the works required by the notice to be executed are otherwise unreasonable in character or extent, or are unnecessary,

(d) that the time within which the works are to be executed is not reasonably sufficient for the purpose,

(e) that the notice might lawfully have been served on the occupier of the premises in question instead of on the owner, or on the owner instead of on the occupier, and that it would have been equitable for it to have been so served,

(f) where the works are works for the common benefit of the premises in question and other premises, that some other person, being the owner or occupier of premises to be benefited, ought to contribute towards the expenses of executing any works required.

(2) If and in so far as an appeal under this section is based on the ground of some informality, defect or error in or in connection with the notice, the court shall dismiss the appeal, if it is satisfied that the informality, defect or error was not a material One.

(3) The appellant—

(a) shall, where the grounds upon which the appeal is brought include a ground specified in subsection (1)(e) or (f) above, serve a copy of his notice of appeal on each other person referred to, and

(b) may, in the case of any appeal under this section, serve a copy of his notice of appeal on any other person having an estate or interest in the premises in question, and on the hearing of the appeal the court may make such order as it thinks fit with respect to—

(i) the person by whom any works are to be executed and the contribution to be made by any other person towards the cost of the works, or

(ii) the proportions in which any expenses that may become recoverable by the local authority are to be borne by the appellant and such other person.

(4) In exercising its powers under subsection (3) above, the court shall have regard—

(a) as between an owner and an occupier, to the terms and conditions, whether contractual or statutory, of the tenancy and to the nature of the works required, and

(b) in any case, to the degree of benefit to be derived by the different persons concerned.

(5) This section has effect subject to any modification specified in the provision under which the notice is given.

General provisions about appeals and applications

103 Procedure on appeal or application to magistrates' court

(1) Where this Act provides—

(a) for an appeal to a magistrates' court against a requirement, refusal or other decision of a local authority, or

(b) for a matter to be determined by, or for an application in respect of a matter to be made to, a magistrates' court,

the procedure shall be by way of complaint for an order.

(2) The time within which such an appeal may be brought is 21 days from the date on which notice of the local authority's requirement, refusal or other decision was served upon the person desiring to appeal, and for the purposes of this subsection the making of the complaint is deemed to be the bringing of the appeal.

(3) In a case where such an appeal lies, the document notifying to the person concerned the local authority's decision in the matter shall state the right of appeal to a magistrates' court and the time within which such an appeal may be brought.

104 Local authority to give effect to appeal

Where upon an appeal under this Act a court varies or reverses a decision of a local authority, it is the duty of the local authority to give effect to the order of the court and, in particular, to grant or issue any necessary consent, certificate or other document, and to make any necessary entry in any register.

105 Judge not disqualified by liability to rates

A judge of a court or a justice of the peace is not disqualified from acting in cases arising under this Act by reason only of his being, as one of several ratepayers, or as one of any other class of persons, liable in common with the others to contribute to, or be benefited by, a rate or fund out of which expenses of a local authority are to be defrayed.

Compensation, and recovery of sums

106 Compensation for damage

(1) A local authority shall make full compensation to a person who has sustained damage by reason of the exercise by the authority, in relation to a matter as to which he has not himself been in default, of any of their powers under this Act.

(2) Subject to subsection (3) below, any dispute arising under this section as to the fact of damage, or as to the amount of compensation, shall be determined by arbitration.

(3) If the compensation claimed does not exceed £50, all questions as to the fact of damage, liability to pay compensation and the amount of compensation may on the application of either party be determined by, and any compensation awarded may be recovered before, a magistrates' court.

107 Recovery of expenses etc.

(1) Where a local authority have incurred expenses for whose repayment the owner of the premises in respect of which the expenses were incurred is liable, either under this Act or by agreement with the authority, those expenses, together with interest from the date of service of a demand for the expenses, may be recovered by the authority—

(a) from the person who is the owner of the premises at the date on which the works are completed, or

(b) if he has ceased to be the owner of the premises before the date on which a demand for the expenses is served, either from him or from the person who is the owner at the date on which the demand is served,

and, as from the date of the completion of the works, the expenses and interest accrued due thereon are, until recovered, a charge on die premises and on all estates and interests in them.

(2) A local authority, for the purpose of enforcing a charge under subsection (1) above, have all the same powers and remedies under the Law of Property Act 1925 and otherwise as if they were mortgagees by deed having powers of sale and lease, Of accepting surrenders of leases and of appointing a receiver.

(3) The rate of interest chargeable under subsection (1) above is such reasonable rate as the authority may determine.

(4) A sum that a local authority are entitled to recover under this Act, and with respect to whose recovery provision is not made by any other section of this Act. may be recovered as a simple contract debt in any court of competent jurisdiction.

(5) Where—

(a) a person has been given a notice in relation to which section 102 above applies, and

(b) the local authority take proceedings against him for the recovery of expenses that they are entitled to recover from him,

it is not open to him to raise any question that he could have raised on an appeal under that section.

108 Payments by instalments

(1) A local authority may by order declare any expenses. recoverable by them under section 107(1) above to be payable with interest by instalments within a period not exceeding 30 years, until the whole amount is paid.

(2) An order may be made under subsection (1) above at any time with respect to an unpaid balance of expenses and accrued interest, but the period for repayment shall not in any case extend beyond 30 years from the service of the first demand for the expenses.

(3) Any such instalments and interest, or any part thereof, may be recovered from the owner or occupier for the time being of the premises in respect of which the expenses were incurred, and, if recovered from the occupier, may be deducted by him from the rent of the premises; but an occupier shall not be required to pay at any one time a sum in excess of the amount that—

(a) was due from him on account of rent at, or

(b) has become due from him on account of rent since,

the date on which he received a demand from the local authority together with a notice requiring him not to pay rent to his landlord without deducting the sum so demanded.

(4) The rate of interest chargeable under subsection (1) above is such reasonable rate as the authority may determine. Inclusion of several sums in one complaint

109 Inclusion of several sums in one complaint

Where two or more sums are claimed from a person as being due under this act or under building regulations, a complaint, summons or warrant issued, for the purposes of that provision or of the building regulations, in respect of that person may contain, in its body or in a schedule, all or any of the sums so claimed.

110 Liability of agent or trustee

Where a local authority claim to recover expenses under this Act from a person as being the owner of the premises in respect of which the expenses were incurred, and that person proves that—

(a) he is receiving the rent of those premises merely as agent or trustee for some other person, and

(b) he has not, and since the date of the service on him of a demand for payment has not had, in his hands on behalf of that other person sufficient money to discharge the whole demand of the authority,

his liability is limited to the total amount of the money that he has or has had in his hands as aforesaid, but a local authority who are, or would be, debarred by the foregoing provisions of this section from recovering the whole of any such expenses from an agent or trustee may recover the whole or any unpaid balance thereof from the person on whose behalf the agent or trustee receives the rent.

111 Arbitration

In an arbitration under this Act, the reference shall be to a single arbitrator appointed by agreement between the parties, or in default of agreement by the Secretary of State.

Obstruction

112 Obstruction

A person who wilfully obstructs a person acting in the execution of this Act, or of building regulations, or of an order or warrant made or issued under this Act, is, in a case for which no other provision is made by this Act, liable on summary conviction to a fine not exceeding level 1 on the standard scale.

Prosecutions

113 Prosecution of offences

Proceedings in respect of an offence created by or under this Act shall not, without the written consent of the Attorney General, be taken by any person other than—

(a) a party aggrieved, or

(b) a local authority or a body whose function it is to enforce the provision in question.

114 Continuing offences

Where provision is made by or under this Act for the imposition of a daily penalty in respect of a continuing offence—

(a) the court by which a person is convicted of the original offence may fix a reasonable period from the date of conviction for the defendant to comply with any directions given by the court, and

(b) where the court has fixed such a period, the daily penalty s not recoverable in respect of any day before the period expires.

Protection of members etc. of authorities

115 Protection of members etc. of authorities

(1) Nothing done, and no contract entered into by a local authority, port health authority or joint board, and nothing done by a member or officer of, or person acting under the direction of, such an authority or board, shall subject them or him personally to any action, liability, claim or demand whatsoever, if it is done or entered into bona fide for the purpose of executing this Act.

(2) Any expense incurred by such an authority, board, member, officer or other person acting bona fide for the purpose aforesaid shall be borne and repaid out of the fund or rate applicable by the authority or board for the general purposes of this Act.

(3) Subsections (1) and (2) above do not exempt a member of such an authority or board from liability to make a payment in pursuance of section 19 or 20 of the Local Government Finance Act 1982 (unlawful expenditure).

Default powers

116 Default powers of Secretary of State

(1) If the Secretary of State is satisfied that a local authority or joint board have failed to discharge their functions under this Act in a case in which they ought to have discharged them, he may make an order declaring them to be in default and directing them for the purpose of removing the default to discharge such of their functions, in such manner and within such time or times, as may be specified in the order.

(2) If a local authority or joint board with respect to whom an order has been made under subsection (1) above fail to comply with a requirement of the order within the time limited by the order for compliance with that requirement, the Secretary of State, in lieu of enforcing the order by mandamus or otherwise, may make an order transferring to himself such of the functions of the body in default as may be specified in his order.

117 Expenses of Secretary of State

(1) Where the Secretary of State has by order under section 116(2) above transferred functions to himself, any expenses incurred by him in discharging those functions shall be paid in the first instance out of moneys provided by Parliament, but the amount of those expenses as certified by the Secretary of State

(a) shall be paid to him by the body in default on demand, and

(b) is recoverable by him from it as a debt due to the Crown, and that body has the like power of raising the money required as it has of raising money for defraying expenses incurred directly by it.

(2) The payment of such expenses as aforesaid is, to such extent as may be sanctioned by the Secretary of State, a purpose for which a local authority or joint board may borrow money in accordance with the statutory provisions relating to borrowing by such an authority or board.

118 Variation or revocation of order transferring powers

(1) Where the Secretary of State has made an order under section 116(2) above, he may at any time by a subsequent order vary or revoke that order, but without prejudice to the validity of anything previously done.

(2) Where an order is so revoked, the Secretary of State may, either by the revoking order or by a subsequent order, make such provision as appears to him to be desirable with respect to the transfer, vesting and discharge of any property or liabilities acquired or incurred by him in discharging functions to which the revoked order related.

Local inquiries

119 Local inquiries

The Secretary of State may cause a local inquiry to be held in a case where he is authorised by this Act to determine a difference, to make an order, to give a consent or approval or otherwise to act under such a provision.

Orders

120 Orders

(1) The power to make an order under section 16(13), 30(3) or (4), 42(7), 69(6) or 134(1) above, or under paragraph 5(2) of Schedule 1 to this Act, is exercisable by statutory instrument, and different days may be appointed by such an order for different provisions or for different purposes.

(2) An order under section 30(3) above or 134(1)(a), (b) or (c) below may contain such transitional provisions and savings as appear to the Secretary of State to be necessary or expedient in connection with the provisions thereby brought into force, including such adaptations of those provisions as appear to him necessary or expedient in consequence of the partial operation of this Act (whether before or after the day appointed by the order).

Interpretation

121 Meaning of " building "

(1) The word " building ", for the purposes of—

(a) Part I of this Act, and

(b) any other enactment (whether or not contained in this Act) that relates to building regulations, or that mentions " buildings " or " a building " in a context from which it appears that those expressions are there intended to have the same meaning as in Part I of this Act,

means any permanent or temporary building, and, unless the context otherwise requires, it includes any other structure or erection of whatever kind or nature (whether permanent or temporary).

(2) In subsection (1) above, " structure or erection " includes a vehicle, vessel, hovercraft, aircraft or other movable object of any kind in such circumstances as may be prescribed (being circumstances that in the opinion of the Secretary of State justify treating it for those purposes as a building).

(3) For the purposes mentioned in subsection (1) above, unless the context otherwise requires—

(a) a reference to a building includes a reference to part of a building, and

(b) a reference to the provision of services, fittings and equipment in or in connection with buildings, or to services, fittings and equipment so provided, includes a reference to the affixing of things to buildings or, as the case may be, to things so affixed.

122 Meaning of " building regulations "

In this Act—

(a) " building regulations" means, subject to paragraph (b) below, regulations made under section 1 above ;

(b) a reference to building regulations, in a particular case in relation to which a requirement of building regulations is for the time being dispensed with, waived, relaxed or modified by virtue of section 8 or 11 above or any other enactment, is a reference to building regulations as they apply in that case, unless the context otherwise requires.

123 Meaning of " construct " and " erect"

(1) For the purposes of—

(a) Part I of this Act, and

(b) any other enactment (whether or not contained in this Act) that relates to building regulations, or that mentions " buildings " or " a building " in a context from which it appears that those expressions are there intended to have the same meaning as in the said Part I,

references to the construction or erection of a building include references to—

(i) the carrying out of such operations (whether for the reconstruction of a building, the roofing over of an open space between walls or buildings, or otherwise) as may be designated in building regulations as operations falling to be treated for those purposes as the construction or erection of a building, and

(ii) the conversion of a movable object into what is by virtue of section 121(1) and (2) above a building,

and " construct " and " erect " shall be construed accordingly.

(2) For the purposes of Part III of this Act, each of the following operations is deemed to be the erection of a building—

(a) the re-erection of a building or part of a building when an outer wall of that building or, as the case may be, that part of a building has been pulled down, or burnt down, to within 10 feet of the surface of the ground adjoining the lowest storey of the building or of that part of the building,

(b) the re-erection of a frame building or part of a frame building when that building or part of a building has been so far pulled down, or burnt down, as to leave only the framework of the lowest storey of the building or of that part of the building,

(c) the roofing over of an open space between walls or buildings,

and " erect " shall be construed accordingly.

124 Meaning of deposit of plans

In this Act, a reference to the deposit of plans in accordance with building regulations is a reference to the deposit of plans in accordance with building regulations for the purposes of section 16 above, unless the context otherwise requires.

125 Construction and availability of sewers

(1) A reference in Part I of this Act to the construction of a sewer includes a reference to the extension of an existing sewer.

(2) For the purposes of sections 64(2) and 66(1) above, a building or proposed building—

(a) is not deemed to have a sufficient water supply available unless—

(i) it has a sufficient supply of water laid on, or

(ii) such a supply can be laid on to it from a point within 100 feet of the site of the building or proposed building, and the intervening land is land through which the owner of the building or proposed building is, or will be, entitled to lay a communication pipe, and

(b) is not deemed to have a sewer available unless—

(i) there is within 100 feet of the site of the building or proposed building, and at a level that makes it reasonably practicable to construct a drain to communicate with it, a public sewer or other sewer that the owner of the building or proposed building is, or will be, entitled to use, and

(ii) the intervening land is land through which he is entitled to construct a drain.

(3) The limit of 100 feet does not apply, for the purposes of subsection (2) above, if the local authority undertake to bear so much of the expenses reasonably incurred in—

(a) constructing, and maintaining and repairing, a drain to communicate with a sewer, or

(b) laying, and maintaining and repairing, a pipe for the purpose of obtaining a supply of water,

as the case may be, as is attributable to the fact that the distance of the sewer, or of the point from which a supply of water can be laid on, exceeds 100 feet.

126 General interpretation

In this Act, unless the context otherwise requires—

" Act" includes an enactment contained in a local Act;

" approved inspector" has the meaning given by section 49(1) above;

" authorised officer", in relation to a local authority, means—

(a) an officer of the local authority authorised by them in writing, either generally or specially, to act in matters of a specified kind or in a specified matter, or

(b) by virtue of his appointment and for the purpose of matters within his province, a proper officer of the local authority or a district surveyor;

" cesspool " includes a settlement tank or other tank for the reception or disposal of foul matter from buildings ;

" closet" includes privy ;

" contravention" includes failure to comply, and " contravene " has a corresponding meaning;

" district surveyor " has the meaning given by section 4 of the London Building Acts (Amendment) Act 1939;

" drain " means a drain used for the drainage of one building or of buildings or yards appurtenant to buildings within the same curtilage, and includes any manholes, ventilating shafts, pumps or other accessories belonging to the drain;

" earth-closet " means a closet having a movable receptacle for the reception of faecal matter and its deodorisation by the use of earth, ashes or chemicals, or by other methods;

" enactment" includes an enactment contained in a local Act;

" factory " has the meaning given by section 175 of the Factories Act 1961 ;

" fire authority " has the meaning given by section 43(1) of the Fire Precautions Act 1971 ;

" functions " includes powers and duties ;

" highway authority " means, in the case of a highway repairable by the inhabitants at large, the council in whom the highway is vested ;

" house " means a dwelling-house, whether a private dwelling-house or not;

" inner London" means the area comprising the inner London boroughs, the City of London, the Inner Temple and the Middle Temple ;

" joint board " has the meaning given by section 343(1) of the Public Health Act 1936 ;

" limits of supply ", in relation to statutory water undertakers, means the limits within which they are for the time being authorised by or under an Act to supply water;

" local Act" includes a provisional order confirmed by Parliament, and the confirming Act so far as it relates to that order;

" local authority " means—

(a) for the purposes of Parts I and II above, and of this Part so far as it relates to them—

(i) a district council,

(ii) the Greater London Council,

(iii) a London borough council,

(iv) the Common Council of the City of London,

(v) the Sub-Treasurer of the Inner Temple, or

(vi) the Under Treasurer of the Middle Temple, and includes the Council of the Isles of Scilly,

(b) for the purposes of Part III above, and of this Part so far as it relates to it—

(i) a district council,
(ii) a London borough council,
(iii) the Common Council of the City of London,
(iv) the Sub-Treasurer of the Inner Temple, or
(v) the Under-Treasurer of the Middle Temple:

" modifications " includes additions, omissions and amendments, and related expressions shall be construed accordingly;

" officer " includes servant;

" owner" means the person for the time being receiving the rackrent of the premises in connection with which the word is used, whether on his own account or as agent or trustee for another person, or who would so receive it if those premises were let at a rackrent;

" plans " includes drawings of any other description, and also specifications or other information in any form;

" prejudicial to health " means injurious, or likely to cause injury, to health;

" premises " includes buildings, land, easements and hereditaments of any tenure;

" prescribed " means prescribed by building regulations ;

" private sewer " means a sewer that is not a public sewer ;

" proper officer ", in relation to a purpose and to a local authority, means an officer appointed for that purpose by that authority;

" public sewer " has the meaning given by section 20 of the Public Health Act 1936 ;

"rackrent", in relation to property, means a rent that is not less than two-thirds of the rent at which the property might reasonably be expected to let from year to year, free from all usual tenant's rates and taxes, and deducting from it the probable average annual cost of the repairs, insurance and other expenses (if any) necessary to maintain the property in a state to command such rent;

"rating district" has the meaning given by section 115(1) of the General Rate Act 1967 ;

" relevant period " has the meaning given by section 16(12) or 81(4) above, as the case may require ;

" sanitary convenience " means closet or urinal;

" school" includes a Sunday school or a Sabbath school;

" sewer " does not include a drain as defined in this section, but otherwise it includes all sewers and drains used for the drainage of buildings and yards appurtenant to buildings, and any manholes, ventilating shafts, pumps or other accessories belonging to the sewer;

" standard scale " has the meaning given by section 75 of the Criminal Justice Act 1982 ;

"statutory maximum'" has the meaning given by section 74of the Criminal Justice Act 1982 ;

" statutory undertakers " means persons authorised by an enactment or statutory order to construct, work or carry on a railway, canal, inland navigation, dock harbour, tramway, gas, electricity, water or other public undertaking;

" statutory water undertakers" means water undertakers who are a company, board, committee or person empowered by or under an Act to supply water;

" street" includes a highway, including a highway over a bridge, and a road, lane, footway, square, court, alley or passage, whether a thoroughfare or not;

" substantive requirements ", in relation to building regulations, means the requirements of building regulations with respect to the design and construction of buildings and the provision of services, fittings and equipment in or in connection with buildings (including requirements imposed by virtue of section 2(1) or (2)(a) Or (b) above), as distinct from procedural requirements;

" surface water " includes water from roofs;

"water-closet" means a closet that has a separate fixed receptacle connected to a drainage system and separate provision for flushing from a supply of clean water either by the operation of mechanism or by automatic action;

" workplace " does not include a factory, but otherwise it includes any place in which persons are employed otherwise than in domestic service.

127 Construction of certain references concerning Temples

In relation to the Inner Temple and the Middle Temple, a reference in a provision of this Part of this Act to the proper officer or an officer or authorised officer of a local authority is a reference to an officer authorised by the Sub-Treasurer or the Under Treasurer, as the case may be, to act for the purposes of that provision.

Savings

128 Protection for dock and railway undertakings

Section 333 of the Public Health Act 1936 applies in relation to local authorities acting under this Act as it applies in relation to local authorities acting under that Act.

129 Saving for Local Land Charges Act 1975

Nothing in this Act about the recovery of expenses from owners of premises affects the Local Land Charges Act 1975.

130 Saving for other laws

All powers and duties conferred or imposed by this Act are in addition to, and not hi derogation of, any other powers and duties conferred or imposed by Act, law or custom, and, subject to any express provision of this Act, all such other powers and duties may be exercised and shall be performed in the same manner as if this Act had not been passed.

131 Restriction of application of Part IV to

This Part has effect subject to paragraph 13 of Schedule 3 to this Act.

PART V

SUPPLEMENTARY

132 Transitional provisions

The transitional provisions contained in Schedule 5 to this Act have effect.

133 Consequential amendments and repeals

(1) The enactments specified in Schedule 6 to this Act have effect subject to the amendments specified in that Schedule.

(2) The enactments specified in Schedule 7 to this Act are repealed to the extent specified in the third column of that Schedule.

134 Commencement

(1) The following provisions of this Act—

(a) section 12, 13,,31, 38, 42(4) to (6) and 43(3), except so far as they enable regulations to be made,

(b) sections 20, 33, 42(1) to (3), 43(1) and (2), 44 and 45,

(c) section 133(2) and Schedule 7 so far as they relate to the Town and Country Planning Act 1947 and the Atomic Energy Authority Act 1954, and

(d) section 50(2) and (3) and paragraph 9 of Schedule 1,

come into force on such day as the Secretary of State may by order appoint.

(2) Subject to—

(a) subsection (1) above, and

(b) sections 16(13) and 42(7) above,

this Act comes into force on 1st December 1984.

135 Short title and extent

(1) This Act may be cited as the Building Act 1984.

(2) This Act does not extend to Scotland or to Northern Ireland.

SCHEDULES

SCHEDULE 1

Section 1(3).

BUILDING REGULATIONS

1 Building regulations may—

(a) provide for particular requirements of the regulations to be deemed to be complied with where prescribed methods of construction, prescribed types of materials or other prescribed means are used in or in connection with buildings,

(b) be framed to any extent by reference to a document published by or on behalf of the Secretary of State or another person or a body, or by reference to the approval or satisfaction of a prescribed person or body.

2 Building regulations may include provision as to—

(a) the giving of notices,

(b) the deposit of plans of proposed work or work already executed (including provision as to the number of copies to be deposited),

(c) the retention by local authorities of copies of plans deposited with them in accordance with the regulations,

(d) the inspection and testing of work,

(e) the taking of samples.

3 Building regulations may provide for requiring local authorities and approved inspectors in prescribed circumstances to consult a prescribed person before taking a prescribed step in connection with any work or other matter to which building regulations are applicable.

4 Building regulations may—

(a) authorise local authorities to accept, as evidence that the requirements of building regulations as to matters of a prescribed description are or would be satisfied, certificates to that effect by persons of a class or description prescribed in relation to those matters or by a person nominated in writing by the Secretary of State in a particular case,

(b) provide for the issue by local authorities of certificates to the effect that, so far as the authority concerned have been able to ascertain after taking all reasonable steps in that behalf, the requirements of building regulations as to matters of a prescribed description are satisfied in a particular case, and for such certificates to be evidence (but not conclusive evidence) of compliance with the regulations,

(c) make provision—

(i) for prohibiting, in prescribed circumstances, the carrying out of proposed work of a prescribed class involving matters of a prescribed description unless there has been deposited with the prescribed authority as regards those matters a certificate such as is mentioned in sub-paragraph (a) above,

(ii) for enabling, in cases where such a certificate is required by virtue of paragraph (i) above, a dispute as to whether a certificate ought to be issued to be referred to the Secretary of State,

(iii) for enabling the Secretary of State, on such a reference, to give such directions as he thinks fit

5 (1) Building regulations may authorise local authorities to charge prescribed fees for or in connection with the performance of prescribed functions of theirs relating to building regulations.

(2) The Secretary of State may by order repeal this paragraph.

6 Building regulations may make a prescribed person or class of persons responsible (instead of local authorities) for performing prescribed functions of local authorities under or in connection with building regulations, and for that purpose may provide for a prescribed enactment relating to building regulations and a prescribed provision of such regulations to apply (with any prescribed modifications) in relation to a prescribed person or a person of a prescribed class as that enactment or provision applies in relation to a local authority.

7 Without prejudice to the generality of section 1(1) of this Act, building regulations may—

(a) for any of the purposes mentioned in section 1 (1) of this Act, make provision with respect to any of the following matters—

(i) preparation of sites,

(ii) suitability, durability and use of materials and components (including surface finishes),

(iii) structural strength and stability, including—

(a) precautions against overloading, impact and explosion,

(b) measures to safeguard adjacent buildings and services,

(c) underpinning,

(iv) fire precautions, including—

(a) structural measures to resist the outbreak and spread of fire and to mitigate its effects,

(b) services, fittings and equipment designed to mitigate the effects of fire or to facilitate fire-fighting,

(c) means of escape in case of fire and means for securing that such means of escape can be safely and effectively used at all material times,

(v) resistance to moisture and decay,

(vi) measures affecting the transmission of heat,

(vii) measures affecting the transmission of sound,

(viii) measures to prevent infestation,

(ix) measures affecting the emission of smoke, gases, fumes, grit or dust or other noxious or offensive substances,

(x) drainage (including waste disposal units),

(xi) cesspools and other means for the reception, treatment or disposal of foul matter,

(xii) storage, treatment and removal of waste,

(xiii) installations utilising solid fuel, oil, gas, electricity or any other fuel or power (including appliances, storage tanks, heat exchangers, ducts, fans and other equipment),

(xiv) water services (including wells and bore-holes for the supply of water) and fittings and fixed equipment associated therewith,

(xv) telecommunications services (including telephones and radio and television wiring installations),

(xvi) lifts, escalators, hoists, conveyors and moving footways,

(xvii) plant providing air under pressure,

(xviii) standards of heating, artificial lighting, mechanical ventilation and air-conditioning and provision of power outlets,

(xix) open space about buildings and the natural lighting and ventilation of buildings,

(xx) accommodation for specific purposes in or in connection with buildings, and the dimensions of rooms and other spaces within buildings,

(xxi) means of access to and egress from buildings and parts of buildings,

(xxii) prevention of danger and obstruction to persons in and about buildings (including passers-by),

(xxiii) matters connected with or ancillary to any of the foregoing matters,

(b) require things to be provided or done in connection with buildings (as well as regulating the provision or doing of things in or in connection with buildings),

(c) prescribe the manner in which work is to be carried out.

8 (1) Building regulations may be made with respect to—

(a) alterations and extensions of buildings and of services, fittings and equipment in or in connection with buildings,

(b) new services, fittings or equipment provided in or in connection with buildings,

(c) buildings and services, fittings and equipment in or in connection with buildings, so far as affected by—

(i) alterations or extensions of buildings, or

(ii) new, altered or extended services, fittings or equipment in or in connection with buildings,

(d) the whole of a building, together with any services, fittings or equipment provided in or in connection with it, in respect of which there are or are proposed to be carried out any operations that by virtue of section 123(1) of this Act constitute the construction of a building for the purposes of this paragraph,

(e) buildings or parts of buildings, together with any services, fittings or equipment provided in or in connection with them, in cases where the purposes for which or the manner or circumstances in which a building or part of a building is used change or changes in a way that constitutes a material change of use of the building or part within the meaning of the expression " material change of use " as defined for the purposes of this paragraph by building regulations.

(2) So far as they relate to matters mentioned in sub-paragraph (1) above, building regulations may be made to apply to or in connection with buildings erected before the date on which the regulations came into force but, except as aforesaid (and subject to section 2(2) of this Act), shall not apply to buildings erected before that date.

9 Building regulations may authorise local authorities, subject to and in accordance with the regulations, to fix by means of schemes and to recover such charges for or in connection with the performance of functions of theirs relating to building regulations as they may determine in accordance with principles prescribed by the regulations.

10 Building regulations may—

(a) provide for a provision thereof to apply generally, or in a particular area,

(b) make different provision for different areas and generally different provision for different circumstances or cases,

(c) include such supplemental and incidental provisions as appear to the Secretary of State expedient.

11 (1) Building regulations may repeal or modify—

(a) any of the following provisions of this Act: sections 15, 18 19, 21 to 29, 41, 59 to 87, 91 to 119, 123(2) and 126 (except as to the definitions of " contravention ", " local authority " paragraph (a), " modifications ", " plans ", " prescribed " and substantive requirements"), and paragraphs 1 and 5 to 14 of Schedule 3, or

(b) any provision of an Act passed before the 20th September 1974,

if it appears to the Secretary of State that it is inconsistent with, or is unnecessary or requires alteration in consequence of, any provision contained in or made under any enactment relating to building regulations.

(2) Building regulations may—

(a) repeal or alter section 12(1) of the Local Government (Miscellaneous Provisions) Act 1976 (byelaws as to supply of heat) or any provision of byelaws in force by virtue of it, and

(b) make any modification of section 12(2) of that Act that the Secretary of State considers is appropriate in consequence of the repeal or alteration.

SCHEDULE 2

Section 9(4).

RELAXATION OF BUILDING REGULATIONS FOR EXISTING WORK

Application of Schedule

1 This Schedule applies to a direction under section 8 of this Act that will affect the application of building regulations to work that has been carried out before the giving of the direction.

Cases where no direction may be given

2 Neither the Secretary of State nor a local authority shall give a direction to which this Schedule applies—

(a) if the local authority have, before the making of the application for the direction, become entitled under section 36(3) of this Act to pull down, remove or alter the work to which the application relates, or

(b) if, when the application is made, there is in force an injunction or other direction given by a court that requires the work to be pulled down, removed or altered.

Suspension of certain provisions while application pending

3 (1) Subject to the following provisions of this Schedule, after the making of an application for a direction to which this Schedule applies, and until the application is withdrawn or finally disposed of, no section 36 notice shall be given as regards the work to which the application relates on the ground that it contravenes the requirement to which the application relates.

(2) If an application for a direction to which this Schedule applies is made less than 12 months after the completion of the work to which the application relates, section 36(4) of this Act does not prevent the giving of a notice as regards that work at any time within a period of 3 months from the date on which the application is withdrawn or finally disposed of.

(3) If an application for a direction to which this Schedule applies is made after a section 36 notice has been given on the ground that the work to which the application relates contravenes the requirement to which the application relates (not being an application prohibited by paragraph 2 of this Schedule), section 36(3) of this Act has effect in relation to that work as if for the reference to the period there mentioned there were substituted a reference to a period expiring 28 days after the application is withdrawn or finally disposed of, or such longer period as a magistrates' court may allow.

(4) Subject to the following provisions of this Schedule, if an application for a direction to which this Schedule applies is made after any person has, in consequence of the carrying out of the work to which the application relates in contravention of building regulations, become liable to a penalty continuing from day to day, the daily penalty is not recoverable in respect of any day after the making of the application and before it is withdrawn or finally disposed of.

(5) In a case where an application is withdrawn or is finally disposed of without any direction being given, the Secretary of State or, as the case may be, the local authority may order that the daily penalty is not recoverable in respect of any day during such further period not exceeding 28 days as may be specified in the order.

4 Paragraph 3(1), (3) and (4) above do not apply to an application that is a repetition, or substantially a repetition, of a previous application under section 8 of this Act.

Saving for criminal liability incurred before making of application

5 The giving of a direction to which this Schedule applies does not affect the liability of a person for an offence committed before the giving of the direction, except so far as that liability depends on the continuation of the offence after the giving of the direction.

Termination of proceedings under section 36 on giving of direction

6 If, before the giving of a direction to which this Schedule applies, a section 36 notice has been given, and the contravention of building regulations by virtue of which the notice was given comes to an end when the direction is given, the local authority is not, after the giving of the direction, entitled to proceed under section 36(3) of this Act by virtue of that notice.

SCHEDULE 3

Sections 46, 88 and 91(2).

INNER LONDON

PART I

APPLICATION OF PART I OF THIS ACT

1 Sections 4, 8 to 10, 16, 18, 21 to 23, 24(1), (2) and (4), 25 to 29. 32,36, 37, 39 and 40 of this Act do not apply to inner London.

2 (1) Where, by section 91(2) above or by building regulations made under paragraph 6 of Schedule 1 to this Act or paragraph 14(1) of this Schedule, local authorities, or a prescribed person or class of persons other than local authorities, are made responsible for—

(a) enforcing, or

(b) performing prescribed functions under or in connection with,

building regulations in force in inner London, then, without prejudice to the said paragraphs 6 and 14(1), building regulations may in that connection provide for any relevant provision to apply (with any prescribed modifications, and notwithstanding paragraph 1 above) in relation to any such authority, person or class of persons as that provision applies in relation to a local authority outside inner London.

(2) In sub-paragraph (1) above, " relevant provision" means any of the following provisions of this Act that may be prescribed for the purposes of sub-paragraph (1) above: sections 4, 8 to 10, 16, 18(1), (4) and (5), 21 to 23,24(1), (2) and (4), 26 to 29, 32, 36, 37, 39 and 40.

3 Without prejudice to the generality of paragraph 11(1) of Schedule 1 to this Act, building regulations may repeal or modify—

(a) any provision of the London Building Acts 1930 to 1939,

(b) any provision of an Act passed before the 20th September 1974, in so far as that provision—

(i) applies to or to any part of inner London, and

(ii) relates to, or to the making of, byelaws for or for any part of inner London with respect to any matter for or in connection with which provision can be made by building regulations, or

(c) any provision of byelaws made or having effect under the said Acts or of any such byelaws as are mentioned in sub-paragraph (b)(ii) above,

if it appears to the Secretary of State that the repeal or, as the case may be, the modification of that provision is expedient—

(i) in consequence of the application of any of sections 61, 62 and 67 of the Public Health Act 1936, sections 4(2), (5), (6) and (7), 5 and 9 of the Public Health Act 1961 and sections 61 to 74 and 76 of the Health and Safety at Work etc. Act 1974 to inner London by virtue of section 70(1) of the said Act of 1974 (which section is repealed by and incorporated in this Act),

(ii) in consequence of paragraph 2 or 14 of this Schedule, or

(iii) in connection with any provision contained in building regulations that apply to or to any part of inner London.

4 Before making any building regulations that provide for the repeal or modification of any such provision the Secretary of State shall (without prejudice to the requirements as to consultation in section 14(3) of this Act) consult the Greater London Council and any other local authority who appear to him to be concerned.

PART II

Application of Part III of this Act

5 Sections 71 to 75, 77 to 83, 85 and 90 of this Act do not apply to inner London.

6 Sections 59 to 61 of this Act do not apply to the Inner Temple or the Middle Temple.

PART III

Building and Drainage of Buildings

7 (1) It is not lawful in an inner London borough—

(a) to erect a house or other building, or

(b) to rebuild a house or other building that has been pulled down to, or to a level below, the floor commonly called the ground floor,

unless—

(i) there are provided to the satisfaction of the borough council drains conforming with the requirements of this paragraph, and

(ii) all such drains and all works and apparatus in connection with them are constructed to the satisfaction of the council and, in particular, are constructed of such materials and size, at such level and with such fall as are approved by the council, and are provided with a water supply.

(2) In an inner London borough it is not lawful to occupy a house or other building that has been erected or rebuilt in contravention of sub-paragraph (1) above or of paragraph 13(1) of Part III of Schedule 9 to the London Government Act 1963.

(3) In order to conform with the requirements of this paragraph, a drain must provide for the drainage of the house or building in connection with which it is required—

(a) into such sewer, situated or intended to be constructed near the house, building or site, as the borough council may direct, or

(b) if no sewer is or will be available for the drainage of the house or building, into such covered cesspool or other place, not being under any house or other building, as the council may direct, and the drains must secure efficient drainage by gravitation at all times and under all conditions of all parts of the house or building, including any areas, water-closets, privies and offices belonging to the house or building.

(4) In rebuilding in an inner London borough a house or building that has been pulled down to, or to a level below, the floor commonly called the ground floor—

(a) the level of the lowest floor of the house or building shall, subject to sub-paragraph (5) below, be raised so far as may be necessary to allow of the construction of such works as are required by this paragraph, and

(b) for that purpose levels shall be taken and determined under the direction of the borough council.

(5) Notwithstanding anything in the foregoing provisions of this paragraph, where it is proposed to erect or rebuild in an inner London borough a house or building at such a level as will not allow of the drainage of all parts of the house or building by gravitation as aforesaid, the borough council may, as respects any part of the house or building that cannot be so drained, either—

(a) allow that part to be constructed so as not to require drainage from it, or

(b) allow that part to be drained by means of such pumping or lifting apparatus as may be provided to the satisfaction of the council,

and any pumping or lifting apparatus provided under this sub-paragraph is deemed to be a drain.

(6) Where separate sewers for the reception of surface water and sewage respectively have been, or are intended to be, provided in a street, the borough council may, in the discharge of their functions under this paragraph in relation to a house or other building that is to be drained into the sewers in that street, require that the house or building be provided with separate drains for discharging surface water and sewage respectively into the appropriate sewers.

(7) A person aggrieved by a direction, requirement or other decision of a borough council under this paragraph may appeal to a magistrates' court.

8 (1) Where in an inner London borough—

(a) a house or other building, whenever erected, is not drained, to the satisfaction of the borough council, by means of a sufficient drain communicating with, and emptying itself into, a sewer, and

(b) a sewer is or will be available for the drainage of the house or building,

the council may, by notice served on the owner of the house or building, impose such requirements as are mentioned in sub-paragraph (2) below.

(2) The requirements that may be imposed by notice under sub-paragraph (1) above are requirements—

(a) to construct a covered drain from the house or building into the said sewer and such connections to the drain as are adequate for the purposes of draining the house or building, including any areas, water-closets, privies and offices belonging to the house or building, and of conveying the sewage from it into the sewer,

(b) to construct the drain and the connections of such materials and size, at such level and with such fall as are adequate for the said purposes,

(c) to provide proper paved or impermeable sloping surfaces for carrying surface water into the drain or any connections to it,

(d) to provide proper sinks, and proper inlets and outlets, syphoned or otherwise trapped, for preventing the emission of effluvia from the drain or any connection to it,

(e) to provide a proper water supply and water-supplying pipes, cisterns and apparatus for scouring the drain and any connections to it, and for causing the drain and any connections to it to convey away the soil,

(f) to provide proper sand traps, expanding inlets and other apparatus for preventing the entry of improper substances into the drain or any connections to it, and

(g) to provide all such other proper works and arrangements as appear to the council or their officers necessary to secure the safe and proper working of the drain and to prevent it from obstructing or otherwise injuring, or impeding the action of, the sewer into which it leads.

(3) Where—

(a) a house or other building in an inner London borough, whenever erected, is without sufficient drainage, and

(b) there is no proper sewer within 200 feet of any part of the house or building,

the borough council may, with a view to making temporary provision for the drainage of the house or building and for the abatement of any nuisance existing in it or caused by it, serve on the owner of the house or building a written notice requiring him—

(i) to construct, elsewhere than under a house and not nearer to any house than the council may direct, a covered watertight cesspool or tank or other suitable receptacle, and

(ii) to construct and lay a covered drain leading from the first mentioned house or building into that cesspool, tank or other receptacle.

(4) Where a borough council have required any works to be executed under the foregoing provisions of this paragraph, the council may, from time to time during the execution of the works, cause them to be inspected, and may by further notice served on the owner of the house or building require such reasonable alterations of them, additions to them or abandonment of parts of them as the council or their officers, with the fuller knowledge afforded by the opening of the ground, consider necessary to secure that the works will be thoroughly effective for their purpose.

(5) Where—

(a) it appears to the council of an inner London borough that a group or block of contiguous houses, or of adjacent detached or semi-detached houses, can more economically or advantageously be drained and improved in combination than separately, and

(b) a sewer of sufficient size is situated, or is about to be constructed, within 100 feet of a part of the group or block,

the council may by order (which they may by order vary or revoke) require that the group or block be drained by a combined operation complying with such of the requirements mentioned in sub-paragraph (2) above as may be specified in the order.

(6) In sub-paragraph (5) above, " house " includes a school and also a factory or other building in which persons are employed and, in relation to a house as so defined, includes its curtilage.

(7) Any person aggrieved by an order made by a borough council under sub-paragraph (5) above may appeal to a magistrates' court.

(8) Sub-paragraphs (5) to (7) above apply to the City of London as if references in them to an inner London borough and its council were references to the City of London and its Common Council.

(9) Sections 99 and 102 of this Act apply in relation to a notice given under sub-paragraph (1) or (3) above.

9 (1) No person shall—

(a) begin to lay or to dig out the foundations of a house or building in an inner London borough, or to rebuild a house or building in an inner London borough, or

(b) begin to make a drain for the purpose of draining directly or indirectly into a sewer under the control of the council of an inner London borough,

unless, at least seven days previously, he has given to the borough council notice of his intention to do so, and if a person begins to lay or dig out the foundations of such a house or building, or to make a drain for the purpose aforesaid, in contravention of this paragraph, he is liable to a fine not exceeding level 1 on the standard scale and to a further fine not exceeding two pounds for every day thereafter until the notice is given.

(2) If a house or building, or a drain for draining directly or indirectly into a sewer under the control of the council of a London borough, or any connections to such a drain, or any works, apparatus or water supply in connection with such a drain, is or are begun, erected, made or provided in an inner London borough in contravention of this Part of this Schedule, the borough council at their option may either—

(a) serve upon the owner of the house or building or of the drain, as the case may be, a notice requiring him to cause the house or building to be demolished or altered, or to cause the drain or the connections or other works and apparatus in connection with it or the water supply to be relaid, remade, altered or added to, as the case may require, or

(b) recover from the person in default, as a debt due from him to the council, a penalty not exceeding five pounds, and a further penalty not exceeding two pounds for every day on which the contravention continues.

(3) Sections 99 and 102 of this Act apply in relation to a notice given under sub-paragraph (2) above.

PART IV

BYELAWS

10 (1) The Greater London Council may make byelaws in relation to the demolition of buildings in the inner London boroughs—

(a) requiring the fixing of fans at the level of each floor of a building undergoing demolition,

(b) requiring the hoarding up of windows in a building from which sashes and glass have been removed,

(c) regulating the demolition of internal parts of buildings before any external walls are taken down,

(d) requiring the placing of screens or mats, the use of water or the taking of other precautions to prevent nuisances arising from dust,

(e) regulating the hours during which ceilings may be broken down and mortar may be shot, or be allowed to fall, into any lower floor,

(f) requiring any person proposing to demolish a building to give to the borough council such notice of his intention to do so as may be specified in the byelaws.

(2) Byelaws under this paragraph may make different provision for different cases, and in particular may provide that, in their application to an area specified in the byelaws, the byelaws shall have effect subject to such modifications or exceptions as may be so specified.

(3) No byelaws under this paragraph shall apply to a building (not being a dwelling-house) belonging to a board carrying on a railway undertaking and used by that board as a part of, or in connection with, that undertaking.

11 The Greater London Council shall make byelaws with respect to sanitary conveniences, ashpits, cesspools and receptacles for dung and their accessories, in connection with buildings in the inner London boroughs, the Inner Temple and the Middle Temple, whenever erected.

12 It is the duty of each local authority to enforce in their area any byelaws under paragraph 10 or 11 above that are in force in their area.

13 Part IV of this Act does not apply in relation to this Part of this Schedule, save that in paragraph 11 above " sanitary conveniences " and " cesspools" have the meanings given by section 126 above.

PART V

ENFORCEMENT OF BUILDING REGULATIONS

14 (1) Building regulations may, to such extent as the Secretary of State thinks fit, make—

(a) local authorities other than the Greater London Council, or

(b) district surveyors,

responsible for the enforcement of building regulations in inner London to the exclusion of the Greater London Council.

(2) Subject to any building regulations made by virtue of sub-paragraph (1) above or paragraph 6 of Schedule 1 to this Act, the functions of enforcing building regulations conferred on local authorities generally by section 91(2) of this Act is not conferred on the council of an inner London borough, the Common Council of the City of London, the Sub-Treasurer of the Inner Temple or the Under Treasurer of the Middle Temple.

SCHEDULE 4

Section 54.

PROVISIONS CONSEQUENTIAL UPON PUBLIC BODY'S NOTICE

Duration of notice

1 (1) A public body's notice comes into force when it is accepted by the local authority, either by notice given within the prescribed period to the public body by which it

was given or by virtue of section 54(3) of this Act, and, subject to paragraph 3(3) below, continues in force until the occurrence of, or the expiry of a prescribed period of time beginning on the date of such event as may be prescribed.

(2) Building regulations may empower a local authority to extend (whether before or after its expiry) any such period of time as is referred to in sub-paragraph (1) above.

Public body's plans certificates

2 (1) Where a public body

(a) is satisfied that plans of the work specified in a public body's notice given by it have been inspected by a servant or agent of the body who is competent to assess the plans,

(b) in the light of that inspection is satisfied that the plans neither are defective nor show that work carried out in accordance with them would contravene any provision of building regulations, and

(c) has complied with any prescribed requirements as to consultation or otherwise,

the body may give to the local authority a certificate in the prescribed form (called a " public body's plans certificate ").

(2) Building regulations may authorise the giving of a public body's notice combined with a public body's plans certificate, and may prescribe a single form for such a combined notice and certificate; and where such a prescribed form is used—

(a) a reference in this Schedule or in any other provision of Part II of this Act to a public body's notice or to a public body's plans certificate includes a reference to that form, but

(b) should the form cease to be in force as a public body's notice by virtue of paragraph 1(1) above, nothing in that paragraph affects the continuing validity of the form as a public body's plans certificate.

(3) A public body's plans certificate—

(a) may relate either to the whole or to part only of the work specified in the public body's notice concerned, and

(b) does not have effect unless it is accepted by the local authority to whom it is given.

(4) A local authority to whom a public body's plans certificate is given;—

(a) may not reject the certificate except on prescribed grounds, and

(b) shall reject the certificate if any of the prescribed grounds exists.

(5) Unless, within the prescribed period, the local authority to whom a public body's plans certificate is given give notice of rejection, specifying the ground or grounds in question, to the public body by which the certificate was given, the authority are conclusively presumed to have accepted the certificate.

(6) If it appears to a local authority by whom a public body's plans certificate has been accepted that the work to which the certificate relates has not been commenced within the period of three years beginning on the date on which the certificate was accepted, the authority may rescind their acceptance of the certificate by notice, specifying the ground or grounds in question, given to the public body.

Public body's final certificates

3 (1) Where a public body is satisfied that any work specified in a public body's notice given by it has been completed, the body may give to the local authority such certificate with respect to the completion of the work and compliance with building regulations as may be prescribed (called a " public body's final certificate ").

(2) Sub-paragraphs (3) to (5) of paragraph 2 above have effect in relation to a public body's final certificate as if any reference in those sub-paragraphs to a public body's plans certificate were a reference to a public body's final certificate.

(3) Where a public body's final certificate has been given with respect to any of the work specified in a public body's notice and that certificate has been accepted by the local authority concerned, the public body's notice ceases to apply to that work, but the provisions of section 48(1) of this Act, as applied by section 54(4), continue, by virtue of this sub-paragraph, to apply in relation to that work as if the public body's notice continued in force in relation to it.

Effects of public body's notice ceasing to be in force

4 (1) This paragraph applies where a public body's notice ceases to be in force by virtue of paragraph 1 above.

(2) Building regulations may provide that if—

(a) a public body's plans certificate was given before the day on which the public body's notice ceased to be in force, and

(b) that certificate was accepted by the local authority (before, on or after that day), and

(c) before that day, that acceptance was not rescinded by a notice under paragraph 2(6) above,

then, with respect to the work specified in the certificate, such of the functions of a local authority referred to in section 48(1) of this Act as may be prescribed for the purposes of this sub-paragraph either are not exercisable or are exercisable only in prescribed circumstances.

(3) If, before the day on which the public body's notice ceased to be in force, a public body's final certificate was given in respect of part of the work specified in the notice and that certificate was accepted by the local authority (before, on or after that day), the fact that the public body's notice has ceased to be in force does not affect the continuing operation of paragraph 3(3) above in relation to that part of the work.

(4) Notwithstanding anything in sub-paragraphs (2) and (3) above, for the purpose of enabling the local authority to perform the functions referred to in section 48(1) of this Act in relation to any part of the work not specified in a public body's plans certificate or final certificate, as the case may be, building regulations may require the local authority to be provided with plans that relate not only to that part but also to the part to which the certificate in question relates.

(5) In any case where this paragraph applies, the reference in subsection (4) of section 36 of this Act to the date of the completion of the work in question has effect, in relation to a notice under subsection (1) of that section, as if it were a reference to the date on which the public body's notice ceased to be in force.

(6) Subject to any provision of building regulations made by virtue of sub-paragraph (2) above, if, before the public body's notice ceased to be in force, an offence under

section 35 of this Act was committed with respect to any of the work specified in that notice, summary proceedings for that offence may be commenced by the local authority at any time within six months beginning with the day on which the functions of the local authority referred to in section 48(1) of this Act became exercisable with respect to the provision of building regulations to which the offence relates.

(7) Any reference in the preceding provisions of this paragraph to section 48(1) of this Act is a reference to that section as applied by section 54(4) of this Act.

Consultation

5 Building regulations may make provision for requiring, in such circumstances as may be prescribed, a public body that has given a public body's notice to consult any prescribed person before taking any prescribed step in connection with any work specified in the notice.

SCHEDULE 5

Section 132.

TRANSITIONAL PROVISIONS

Joint application to the Secretary of State for the determination of certain questions relating to building regulations

1 After the date on which section 30 of this Act ceases to have effect by virtue of an order made under subsection (4) of that section, that section continues to apply in relation to an application referred to the Secretary of State under that section before that date.

The Clean Air Act 1956 and the Housing Act 1957

2 Notwithstanding the repeal by this Act of Schedule 1 to the Public Health Act 1961, the amendments made by Part III of that Schedule to the Clean Air Act 1956 and the Housing Act 1957 continue to have effect.

Repeal and amendment of Acts etc.

3 Any power that is exercisable by virtue of—

(a) section 317 of the Public Health Act 1936,

(b) section 82 of the Public Health Act 1961,

(c) section 82, 83 or 84 of the London Government Act 1963,

(d) section 252 or 254 of the Local Government Act 1972, or

(e) section 48 of the Local Government (Miscellaneous Provisions) Act 1982,

in relation to a provision that is repealed and re-enacted by this Act is exercisable in relation to that provision as so re-enacted to the extent to which it would have been exercisable immediately before such repeal.

4 (1) Section 64(5) of the Act of 1936, in so far as it relates to the retention of plans or other documents by a local authority, continues to have effect (notwithstanding its repeal by the Act of 1974) as respects documents deposited in duplicate in pursuance of existing regulations until regulations with respect to the retention by local authorities

of copies of deposited plans have been made under paragraph 2(c) of Schedule 1 to this Act and apply in relation to the documents so deposited.

(2) In this paragraph—

" the Act of 1936 " means the Public Health Act 1936 ;

" the Act of 1961 " means the Public Health Act 1961 ;

" the Act of 1974 " means the Health and Safety at Work etc. Act 1974;

" existing regulations " means regulations made under section 4 of the Act of 1961 that, on the coming into force of the provisions specified in the Schedule to the Health and Safety at Work etc. Act 1974 (Commencement No. 4) Order 1977, had effect in accordance with section 61(6) of the Act of 1974 whether in the form in which they accordingly had effect or as amended.

5 Without prejudice to the power to make building regulations, the repeal of section 70(1) of the Health and Safety at Work etc. Act 1974, and the re-enactment in this Act of that subsection down to " Wales ", do not of themselves cause any building regulations to apply to inner London that were prevented by that subsection from so applying.

SCHEDULE 6

Section 133(1).

Consequential Amendments

The Restriction of Ribbon Development Act 1935

1 In section 17(1) of the Restriction of Ribbon Development Act 1935, after " byelaw " there is inserted " or building regulations " .

The Public Health Act 1936

2 In section 6(1) of the Public Health Act 1936, after the words " except section 46," (which with other words were inserted by the Public Health (Control of Disease) Act 1984) there is inserted " or of the Building Act 1984, " .

3 In section 269(8)(i) of that Act, for " the building byelaws of the local authority " there is substituted " building regulations " .

The Atomic Energy Authority Act 1954

4 In section 5(5) of the Atomic Energy Authority Act 1954, for " Section 71 of the Public Health Act 1936 " there is substituted " Section 4 of the Building Act 1984 " .

The Clean Air Act 1956

5 In section 10(2) of the Clean Air Act 1956, for " subsection (2) of section 64 of the Public Health Act 1936 " there is substituted " section 16(6) of the Building Act 1984 " .

The Housing Act 1957

6 In section 15(1)(b) of the Housing Act 1957, after " 1936," there is inserted " or the Building Act 1984, " .

The Radioactive Substances Act 1960

7 At the end of Part I of Schedule 1 to the Radioactive Substances Act 1960, there is inserted—

"8D Section 59 of the Building Act 1984.".

The Public Health Act 1961

8 In section 17(15) of the Public Health Act 1961 (as substituted by section 27(1) of the Local Government (Miscellaneous Provisions) Act 1982), for "section 39 of the Public Health Act 1936 " there is substituted " section 59 of the Building Act 1984 " .

The London Government Act 1963

9 In paragraph 19 of Part I of Schedule 11 to the London Government Act 1963, for " Sections 87 and 88, in their " there is substituted " Section 87, in its " .

10 In paragraph 9(5) of Part II of Schedule 11 to that Act, for " section 27 of the Public Health Act 1961 " there is substituted " section 79 of the Building Act 1984" .

The Offices, Shops and Railway Premises Act 1963

11 In section 9(6) of the Offices, Shops and Railway Premises Act 1963, for " sections 44 to 46 " there is substituted " section 45 " .

The Faculty Jurisdiction Measure 1964

12 In section 2(4) of the Faculty Jurisdiction Measure 1964—

(a) in paragraph (i), for " section 58 of the Public Health Act 1936 " there is substituted " section 77 of the Building Act 1984 " ;

(b) in paragraph (iii), for " section 25 of the Public Health Act 1961 " there is substituted " section 78 of the Building Act 1984 ";

(c) in paragraph (iv), for " section 27 of the Public Health Act 1961 " there is substituted " section 79 of the Building Act 1984 " .

The Fire Precautions Act 1971

13 For section 30(3)(a) and (b) of the Fire Precautions Act 1971 there is substituted—

"(a) section 71(1) to (4) of the Building Act 1984 ;

(b) section 72 (except subsection (5)) of that Act;".

The Local Government Act 1972

14 In section 181(2)(a) of the Local Government Act 1972, for " sections 14 to 42 " there is substituted " sections 15, 17 to 24, 27, 29 to 34, 36 and 42 " .

The Safety of Sports Grounds Act 1975

15 In section 9(1)(c) of the Safety of Sports Grounds Act 1975, for "section 59 of the Public Health Act 1936" there is substituted " sections 24 and 71 of the Building Act 1984 " .

The Local Land Charges Act 1975

16 In section 1(1)(a) of the Local Land Charges Act 1975, after the words " by that Act)" (which with other words were inserted by the Highways Act 1980) there is inserted " or the Building Act 1984" .

The Local Government (Miscellaneous Provisions) Act 1976

17 In section 12(3) of the Local Government (Miscellaneous Provisions) Act 1976, for the words from "Building regulations" to " alteration; and" there is substituted " Subsections (1) and (2) above have effect subject to paragraph 11(2) of Schedule 1 to the Building Act 1984 ; and " .

The Development of Rural Wales Act 1976

18 In paragraph 51(3) of Schedule 3 to the Development of Rural Wales Act 1976—

(a) after " Public Health Act 1961" there is inserted " or of the Building Act 1984 " , and

(b) after " and 1961" there is inserted " and 1984 " .

The Interpretation Act 1978

19 In Schedule 1 to the Interpretation Act 1978, in the definition of " Building regulations ", for the words from " means " to the end there is substituted " has the meaning given by section 122 of the Building Act 1984 " .

The Highways Act 1980

20 In section 168(1)(b) of the Highways Act 1980, for " section 25 of the Public Health Act 1961 " there is substituted " section 78 of the Building Act 1984 " .

21 In section 223(1)(a) of that Act, for " section 66 of the Public Health Act 1936 " there is substituted " section 32 of the Building Act 1984 " .

New Towns Act 1981

22 In section 34(3) of the New Towns Act 1981—

(a) after " Public Health Act 1961" there is inserted " or of the Building Act 1984 " ;

(b) in paragraph (a), after "Acts" there is inserted " for the purposes of those provisions " ;

(c) for " and 1961 " there is substituted " , 1961 and 1984 " .

The Public Health (Control of Disease) Act 1984

23 There is added at the end of section 7(4) of the Public Health (Control of Disease) Act 1984—

"(k) the Building Act 1984 (other than Parts III of Schedule 3)."

SCHEDULE 7

Section 133(3).

Repeals

Chapter	Short Title	Extent of Repeal
26 Geo. 5 & 1 Edw. 8. c. 49.	Public Health Act 1936.	Section 25.
		Sections 37 to 41.
		Sections 43 and 44.
		Sections 46 and 47.
		Sections 53 to 62.
		Sections 64 to 67.
		Sections 70 and 71.
		Section 88.
		Section 90 (3) and (6).
		Sections 137 and 138.
		Section 142.
		Section 344.
7 & 8 Geo. 6. c. 31.	Education Act 1944.	Section 63(1).
8 & 9 Geo. 6. c. 42.	Water Act 1945.	Sections 29 and 30.
		In Schedule 4, the seventh paragraph.
10 & 11 Geo. 6. c. 51.	Town and Country Planning Act 1947.	In Schedule 8, the amendment of the Public Health Act 1936.
2 & 3 Eliz. 2. c. 32.	Atomic Energy Authority Act 1954.	Section 5(5).
8 & 9 Eliz. 2. c. 34.	Radioactive Substances Act 1960.	In Schedule 1, in paragraph 3 the word " thirty-nine,".
9 & 10 Eliz, 2, c. 64.	Public Health Act 1961.	Sections 4 to 11.
		Sections 19 to 21.
		Sections 23 to 33.
		Schedule 1.
1963 c. 33.	London Government Act 1963.	In Schedule 9, in Part II paragraph 18, and in Part III paragraphs 13 to 15.

Chapter	Short Title	Extent of Repeal
		In Schedule 11, in Part I, in paragraph 11 the words ", section 41 of this Act", paragraphs 12, 21 and 34 to 36, and in Part II paragraphs 2 and 3.
1967 c. xx.	Greater London Council (General Powers) Act 1967.	Section 25.
1971 c. 40.	Fire Precautions Act 1971.	Sections 13(5), 15, 30(1) and 40(7).
1972 c. 70.	Local Government Act 1972.	In Schedule 14, in paragraph 4 the words "41, 46,", and paragraph 10.
1973 c. 37.	Water Act 1973.	Section 14(6) and (7).
		In Schedule 8, in paragraph 36, in sub-paragraph (1)(a) the words from " and sections " to " Middle Temple) ", sub-paragraph (1)(b), and in sub-paragraph (2) the words from " except" to the end, and paragraphs 38, 41 and 42.
1974 c. 37.	Health and Safety at Work etc. Act 1974.	Sections 61 to 74.
		Section 76.
		Schedules 5 and 6.
		In Schedule 10, the items relating to the Public Health Act 1936, the Town and Country Planning Act 1947, the Atomic Energy Authority Act 1954, the Public Health Act 1961, the Airports Authority Act 1965 and the Civil Aviation Act 1971.
1974 c. 40.	Control of Pollution Act 1974.	Section 28(2).
		In section 61(2), the words " under Part II of the Public Health Act 1936 ".
		In Schedule 2, paragraph 10.
1975 c. 78.	Airports Authority Act 1975.	Section 19(2).
1976 c. 57.	Local Government (Miscellaneous Provisions) Act 1976.	Section 34.

Chapter	Short Title	Extent of Repeal
1977 c. 45.	Criminal Law Act 1977.	In Schedule 6, the entries relating to offences under sections 60(1) and 59(4) of the Public Health Act 1936.
1977 c. xv.	City of London (Various Powers) Act 1977.	Section 25.
1980 c. 20.	Education Act 1980.	In sections 14(4) and 27(5), the words " section 71(a) of the Public Health Act 1936 and ".
1980 c. 66.	Highways Act 1980.	Section 112(8).
		In section 114(4), the words from " and nothing " to the end of the subsection.
1981 c. 12.	Water Act 1981.	Section 5.
1982 c. 16.	Civil Aviation Act 1982.	In Schedule 2, paragraph 1(1).
1982 c. 30.	Local Government (Miscellaneous Provisions) Act 1982.	Section 8(1).
		Sections 24 and 25.
		Section 28.
1984 c. 29.	Housing and Building Control Act 1984.	Sections 39 to 59.
		Section 60(2)(b).
		Section 61.
		In section 62(1), the definitions of " contravention" and " local authority ".
		Section 62(2).
		Section 66(2).
		In section 66(3), the words " Except as provided by subsection (2) above,".
		Schedules 8 to 10.
		In Schedule 11, paragraphs 4, 5 and 35.
		In Schedule 12, in Part II, the items relating to section 67 of the Public Health Act 1936 and section 62(3) of the Health and Safety at Work etc. Act 1974.

GRANGIS - UK PUBLISHING 2022.

www.ingramcontent.com/pod-product-compliance
Lightning Source LLC
LaVergne TN
LVHW060213210926
848481LV00008B/2720
* 9 7 9 8 8 8 5 5 9 0 5 3 2 *